LUISA

NOW AND THEN

CAROLE MAUREL

LUISA

NOW AND THEN

ADAPTED BY
MARIKO TAMAKI

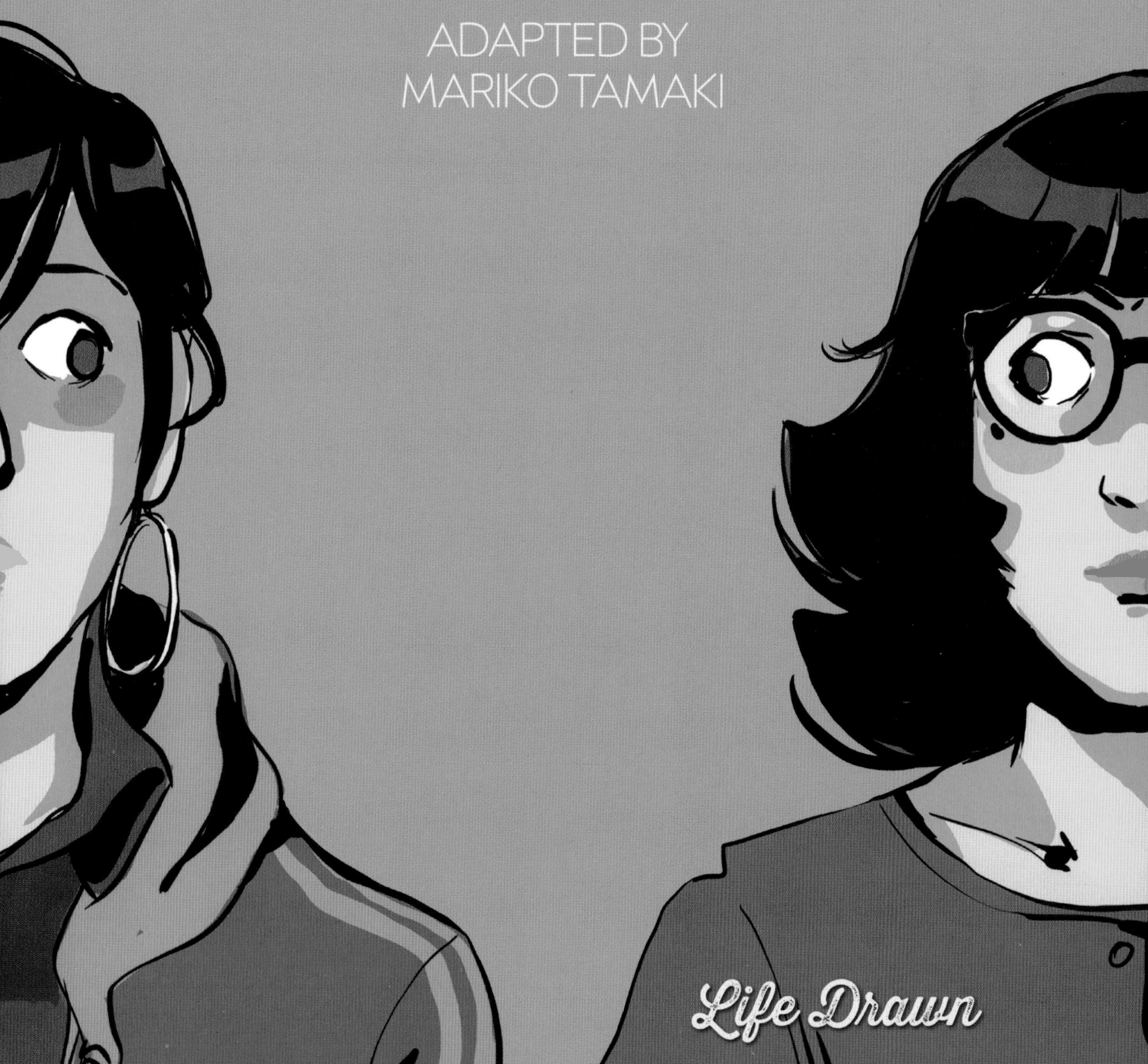

Life Drawn

CAROLE MAUREL
Story & Art

•

MARIKO TAMAKI
English-Language Adaptation

NANETTE McGUINNESS
Translation

•

FABRICE SAPOLSKY
& **ALEX DONOGHUE**
U.S. Edition Editors

VINCENT HENRY
Original Edition Editor

JERRY FRISSEN
Senior Art Director

FABRICE GIGER
Publisher

Rights & Licensing - licensing@humanoids.com
Press and Social Media - pr@humanoids.com

LUISA, NOW AND THEN
This title is a publication of Humanoids, Inc. 8033 Sunset Blvd. #628, Los Angeles, CA 90046.

Life Drawn is an imprint of Humanoids, Inc.

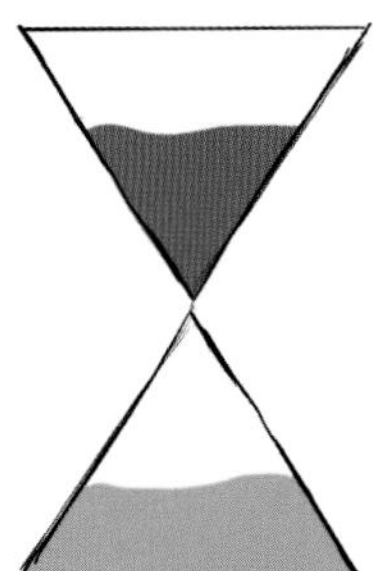

CLICK!

END OF THE LINE...

END OF THE LINE!

YOUNG LADY! EVERYBODY OUT!

BUT...

WHERE ARE WE?

YOUR STOP...

SO, OUT... NOW!

WAIT.
WHAT?

WHERE
AM I?
Chemin Vert

IT'S FINALLY NICE OUT! LET'S SIT IN THE SUN!
UGH. FINE.

SO. IT'S OVER WITH THE NEW GUY?

WHAT WAS IT...? FRANCIS? FABIAN?
FABIAN... IT LASTED A WEEK. SO MUCH FOR FINDING MR. RIGHT.

I DIDN'T EVEN HAVE TIME TO FALL IN LOVE.
YOU'RE TOO PICKY. JUST HAVE SEX!

YOU KNOW WHAT? IF IT'S PICKY TO WANT TO LOVE THE PERSON YOU'RE SLEEPING WITH...

LUISA, NOT TO BE RUDE, BUT YOU CHANGE RELATIONSHIPS WITH THE *SEASONS*.
SO...

HOW DO YOU EXPECT TO MAKE A REAL CONNECTION?

I'M *BORED*, FARID.
YOU'RE RIGHT. WHERE IS THAT WAITER?

NO, I'M BORED WITH GUYS. WHOEVER IT IS, IT'S STILL THE SAME OLD *SAME OLD*...

IN THE BEGINNING, IT'S ALWAYS *SUPER*... *MAGICAL!* WE DO *TONS* OF THINGS TOGETHER...

THEN THEY WANT A *COMMITMENT*, WE MOVE IN TOGETHER, ROUTINE SETS IN, AND I FEEL *SUFFOCATED*...

NO MORE *PASSION*, NO MORE *DESIRE*...
IT'S THE SAME THING EVERY TIME.

IT MAKES ME QUESTION MYSELF...
WHAT'LL YOU HAVE?

A FRIENDLY SERVER! AT LAST! IT'S A MIRACLE!

IGNORE HIM. WE'LL HAVE TWO BEERS!

UH OKAY, YOU CAN HAVE TWO BEERS!
I'LL HAVE A COKE, THANKS VERY MUCH!

A COKE? ARE YOU SICK?
I GOT SO WASTED LAST NIGHT AT ISA...

YOU KNOW, YOU TURN 30, THERE ARE THINGS YOUR BODY CAN'T HANDLE ANYMORE.

I WAS TALKING ABOUT THAT YESTERDAY WITH...
ONE PINT AND ONE COKE FOR TABLE TWELVE!

IF THAT GUY THINKS HE'S GETTING A TIP HE'S DREAMING.

WE'RE BECOMING *OLD FARTS*, FARID...
NAAH!

le Cosy
le Cosy
IT'S NOT JUST THE ALCOHOL...
IT'S PEOPLE. THE STUPIDITY OF PEOPLE!

OH HEY! THAT REMINDS ME!
MMM?

I GOT YOU A DVD!

IT'S SO BEAUTIFUL. IT MADE ME NOSTALGIC.
Camille Redouble

FOR WHAT? ADOLESCENCE AND CONSTANT ANXIETY?

"WILL I BEAT THE CURVE THIS TRIMESTER IN HISTORY? WILL THAT CUTE GUY IN CLASS *FINALLY* TALK TO ME?"

YEAH... I MEAN, I WAS PRETTY TORMENTED AT THAT AGE...
JUST IMAGINE...
IF YOU HAD A CHANCE TO TALK TO TEEN YOU...

WHAT WOULD YOU SAY?

I DUNNO... SOMETHING REASSURING, I GUESS...

HAHAHA! DAMN! POOR KID!

YOU'D BE LIKE, "WELL. AS AN ADULT I'VE DATED A STRING OF GUYS, THAT I DON'T GIVE A FIG ABOUT. THAT I'M NOT INTERESTED IN MARRYING...
...AND I TAKE PICTURES OF FROZEN PIZZAS FOR A LIVING!"

SCREW YOU...

YOU COULD TELL HER THAT IN HER FUTURE, SHE'LL HAVE AMAZING FRIENDS TO CHEER HER UP...

OKAY, I NEED TO GET HOME...
ALREADY?
YOU GONNA CALL UP "TEENAGE YOU"?

THAT'S RIGHT. I'M GOING TO TELL HER LAST MONTH'S WINNING LOTTERY NUMBERS...

NO, I NEED TO CLEAN UP MY PLACE.
THEN I NEED TO HAVE A CHAT WITH MY NEW NEIGHBOR...

THE MUSICIAN? THE PIANIST?
SHE CUTE?

SHE'S TOO YOUNG FOR *YOU!*
ALSO, FOR THE LAST MONTH, SHE'S DECIDED TO START DRILLING AT 10PM EVERY NIGHT!
THAT SUCKS.

I'M OVER HER IKEA-SPONSORED PERCUSSION SESSIONS!

WOOOW, DIY!
YEAH. AND SHE'S KEEPING ME AWAKE.

WELL, SEE YOU SUNDAY NIGHT!
YEP. TAKE CARE!

Beauty

Chemin Ve

11e
Boulevar
VOLTAI

I'M IN PARIS?
HOW AM I IN PARIS?

CARD NOT ACCEPTED
1
2
3

"NOT ACCEPTED?", SERIOUSLY?

GAH!

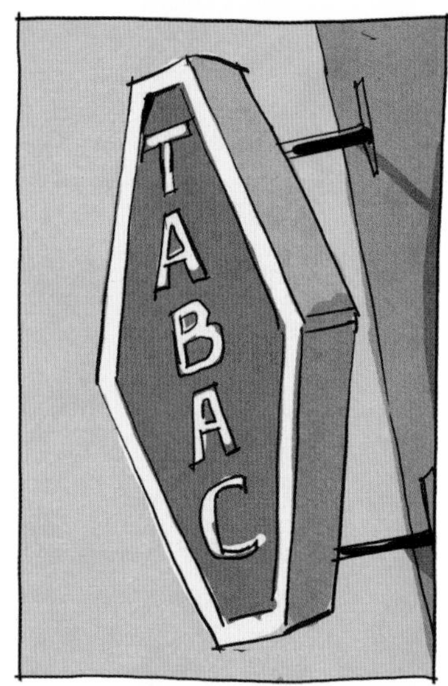
TABAC

HELLO. WHAT CAN I DO FOR YOU, YOUNG LADY?
HELLO, SIR.
LOTO

I...UM...
I'D LIKE A
PHONE CARD.

MINE ISN'T
WORKING AND
I *REALLY* NEED
TO CALL MY
MOTHER...

YOU NEED
A CARD?
YOUR PARENTS
DIDN'T GET YOU
A *SMARTPHONE*
FOR
CHRISTMAS?

HEH, GEORGE!
GET A LOAD
OF THIS!
NO PHONE!
AN *ENDANGERED
SPECIES*, I'M
TELLING YOU!

SORRY ABOUT
THAT! I'VE NEVER
HAD TO SELL A
PHONE CARD
TO A KID...

THAT'LL BE
5.50 EURO...
AND IT'S
RECHARGEABLE.
EURO?

*IN **2002**, THE EURO BECAME FRANCE'S CURRENCY REPLACING THE FRENCH FRANC.

DO YOU NEED HELP?
THE KID IS CLEARLY LOST.
WHERE *EXACTLY* ARE YOU FROM, KID?

A TOWN IN THE BOONIES NEAR CHARTRES...LE COUDRAY.
SHIT. THEY'RE STILL USING FRANCS IN LE COUDRAY?!

COME ON, I'LL BUY YOU A PHONE CARD.

HERE YOU GO...

GEEZ. YOU COULD AT LEAST THANK THE LADY...

NEXT TIME, JUST BEG INSTEAD OF TRYING TO BULLSHIT EVERYONE!

Les Amis
Les Amis
FORGET THAT PLACE.
DON'T LISTEN TO THAT LOSER.

LET'S CALL YOUR HOUSE...
DO YOU KNOW YOUR NUMBER?

UH. I CAN CALL MYSELF!
THANKS FOR THE CARD.

SAVE IT. I'LL USE MY CELL PHONE...

HEY. IS THAT A PAGER?

A PAGER?

UH...NO, IT'S JUST A CELL PHONE...
OKAY. SO WHAT'S YOUR PARENTS' NUMBER?

* FRENCH PHONE NUMBERS WENT FROM 8 TO 10 DIGITS IN 1996.

WHICH MEANS... EITHER YOU'RE A LIAR...

...OR MAYBE, I DON'T KNOW, ARE YOU HAVING A A BREAKDOWN OF SOME KIND?

WELL?

SO WHAT'S GOING ON?
YOU COME FROM CHARTRES? HOW DID YOU GET HERE?

A BUS DROPPED ME OFF ...
WHAT?
WITH *NO* CONNECTIONS?

LOOK, KID, IF YOU WANT ME TO HELP YOU...
...YOU NEED TO TELL ME THE TRUTH.

OKAY!
MY NAME'S LUISA ARAMBOL. I'M 15 YEARS OLD. YESTERDAY NIGHT I TOOK A BUS TO GO *HOME*. I FELL ASLEEP AND WHEN I WOKE UP, THE BUS DROPPED ME OFF *HERE*. MY MONEY'S *WORTHLESS* AND MY MOTHER'S GOING TO *KILL* ME IF I'M NOT HOME BY 8 P.M.
THAT'S THE TRUTH! AND I *DON'T* WANT YOUR HELP!

WHAT A NIGHTMARE!
CRAP!

OKAY. WELL, I'M DELIGHTED TO BE PART OF THIS NIGHTMARE...

I'M SASHA...

...

WHAT WOULD YOU SAY TO A HOT CHOCOLATE?
YOU CAN TELL ME ALL ABOUT IT ...CALMLY.

AND WE'LL TRY TO FIND YOUR PARENTS.

DO YOU HAVE ANY FAMILY IN PARIS?
MY AUNT AURELIA!
SHE'S GOT THE SAME LAST NAME AS ME, "ARAMBOL."

AND SHE LIVES NEAR THE BASTILLE AREA, I THINK...
OKAY, THERE YOU GO!

I'M SURE WE CAN FIND YOUR AUNT. WE'RE IN THE 11TH DISTRICT!

YEAH BUT THE LAST TIME I WAS HERE, I WAS, LIKE, *FIVE*...

I'LL *NEVER* RECOGNIZE HER!
DON'T BE SILLY...

77
SHE'LL RECOGNIZE YOU!

GO ON UP TO THE FIFTH FLOOR. I'LL BE THERE IN A SEC. I JUST HAVE TO PICK UP THE MAIL.
OKAY.

GAH! MOM'S GOING TO *KILL* ME!

I'M SO *DEAD!*

WOW, THIS NEIGHBOR THING JUST KEEPS GETTING *BETTER AND BETTER!*

FUCK, THIS SUCKS!

NOW SHE'S BRINGING KIDS IN TO PUT UP HER SHELVES...

ARAMBOL

ARAMBOL

HEY, KID, GUESS WHAT?
MMMH?

I HOPE YOU BOUGHT A *LOTTERY TICKET* TODAY ...
...BECAUSE YOU ARE A *LUCKY DUCK*!

SOMEONE IN THIS BUILDING HAS THE SAME LAST NAME AS YOU AND YOUR AUNT!
YOU THINK IT'S *HER*?

DO YOU KNOW HER *EXACT* ADDRESS?
NO.
THEN WE'LL FIND OUT.

RRRRRiiiiiiiiii

RRiiiiiiiiNNG
RiiiiiiiiiNG
OKAY, OKAY! I'M COMING!

NO NAME UNDER THE DOORBELL...
COULD STILL BE THOUGH.

YES...?
UMMM...HI, EXCUSE ME.
WE'RE LOOKING FOR SOMEONE WITH THE LAST NAME ARAMBOL...

YES...
AND?

I'VE
GOT THIS KID
WITH ME, SHE'S
LOOKING FOR HER
AUNT, AN AURELIA
ARAMBOL...
DO YOU
KNOW HER?
IS IT YOU?

...

OH,
SHIT!

EXCUSE
ME?
UH,
YES...
NO...

ACTUALLY,
AURELIA ARAMBOL
LIVED HERE TEN
YEARS AGO...
BUT THAT
WAS LONG BEFORE
I MOVED IN.

AND BEFORE SHE *KICKED* THE BUCKET...

YOU KNEW HER?
YES... SHE WAS MY AUNT, TOO...

AND...I...

BLAM

EXCUSE ME!
DO YOU KNOW THIS YOUNG WOMAN?
IS SHE YOUR COUSIN? YOUR NIECE?

I DON'T KNOW *ANYTHING* ABOUT HER!
GO AWAY!

OKAY...

WOW. I'M SORRY, LUISA... I DON'T KNOW WHAT TO SAY...

THERE *HAS* TO BE *ANOTHER* AURELIA ARAMBOL...
IT'S NOT POSSIBLE!

AROUND HERE? FRANKLY, I DOUBT IT...
IT'S BEEN *TEN YEARS* SINCE YOU'VE SEEN HER? *THAT* LONG...?

...

OKAY, YOU KNOW WHAT, LET'S GO INSIDE...

WHAT?! IS THIS YOUR TV OR YOUR COMPUTER?
MY COMPUTER... BUT I WATCH TV ON IT.

CRAZY. PARIS IS SO HIGH TECH.

I DIDN'T EVEN KNOW ANY OF THIS STUFF EXISTED!

REALLY? IT'S LIKE, THE BARE NECESSITIES.

I GUESS...

MAKE YOURSELF AT HOME. HAVE A SEAT.
I WANT TO TALK ABOUT...YOUR STORY. WHICH, I HAVE TO SAY, IS REALLY ODD.

LIKE, I JUST DON'T GET...

I MEAN, MY NEIGHBOR REALLY *LOOKS* JUST LIKE YOU.

MAYBE YOU'RE COUSINS OR SOMETHING.
AND SHE DOESN'T KNOW IT.

DUNNO... MAYBE...
I MEAN, LOOK, IT'S NOT A BIG DEAL.

WE'LL FIGURE IT OUT...
WE'LL *HAVE* TO FIGURE SOMETHING OUT, SINCE I WON'T BE HERE THIS WEEKEND.

SO YOU CAN'T STAY HERE...

1995

NO!

TiLiLiLiLiT
TiLiLiLiLiiiT
TiLiLiLiLiiT

MMMMHMM...
TILILILI LILILI

AREN'T YOU GOING TO ANSWER THAT?
I GOT IT!

OH LOOK! IT'S A GHOST!
WHO IS IT?

SHHH...! LUISA? IS THAT YOU?
THE LAST TIME I HEARD FROM YOU WE WERE USING THE *FRANC*, RIGHT?

HAS SOMETHING HAPPENED TO MOM?
UH, NO...?
THEN WHY ARE YOU CALLING ME?

A COUSIN? I DON'T KNOW... IT'S BEEN YEARS SINCE WE'VE HEARD ANYTHING FROM UNCLE JOHN. I THOUGHT HE ONLY HAD TWO SONS.
AURELIA?

SHE'S BEEN PUSHING UP DAISIES FOR A LONG TIME. OKAY...
THAT'S IT... NO CHILD, NO...

OH YEAH? WHY'S SHE LOOKING FOR AUNTIE AURELIA?
WHO IS SHE?

HEY, WHAT THE HELL, I'M NOT THE ONE WHO INHERITED THE APARTMENT. JUST FIND OUT!
WHAT DOES SHE WANT?

IT'S MY SIS. SHE THINKS WE HAVE A SECRET SISTER OR SOMETHING...

WHAT IN THE WORLD?
SHH, JUST A SEC...

LUISA, THAT'S *IMPOSSIBLE*. DAD DIED IN 1986.
WE *CAN'T* HAVE A SISTER THAT YOUNG!

JUST TALK TO HER. SORT IT OUT!
I HAVE TO GO!

HEY!

DAADDY'S OFF THE PHOOONE! DAADDYY'S OFF THE PHOOONE!

...

I PUT SOME CLEAN TOWELS ON THE SINK FOR YOU...
AND A T-SHIRT...

IS THAT OKAY?
YES, YES! THANKS!

POOR KID...
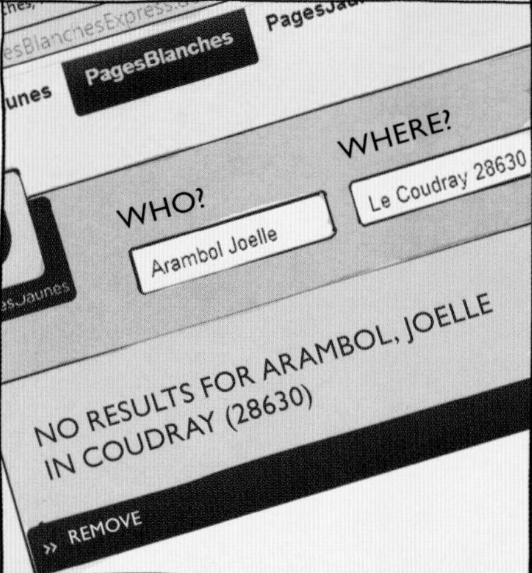
PagesBlanches
PagesJaunes
WHO?
WHERE?
Arambol Joelle
Le Coudray 28630
NO RESULTS FOR ARAMBOL, JOELLE IN COUDRAY (28630)
» REMOVE

WHAT'S ALL THIS JUNK...?

STAR Club
SPECIAL
Beverly Hills
2 SUPER POSTERS

2 SUPER POSTERS

SPECIAL
94-95

DIARY 94-95

OH!

WEDNESDAY
APRIL
12TH
Lucie + Luisa
Contrôle d
exo 5 p 12
français
p 102

DIARY
94-95

HEY!
DIARY
94-95

WHAT'S SHE *DOING*?!
WHAT? WHO?

YOUR *NEIGHBOR*! OVER THERE!

I CAN'T BELIEVE IT! SHE'S LIKE, *OGLING* ME!

HAHAHA! NO. DON'T WORRY...
I DON'T THINK YOU'RE HER TYPE...

YOU KNOW, I THINK SHE KNOWS YOU. BUT IT SEEMS LIKE IT BOTHERS HER OR SOMETHING...

I HAVE A FEELING SHE TOLD US A PACK OF LIES EARLIER...
OH YEAH, SO WHAT'S ALL THIS STUFF IN YOUR BACKPACK?

DID YOU HIT A *FLEA MARKET* BEFORE YOU CAME HERE, OR SOMETHING?
SPECIAL
DON'T TOUCH THAT!

THAT'S MINE!
OKAY... OKAY!

ALRIGHT... WELL, IT'S GETTING LATE...

LET'S GET A BITE TO EAT...
WE'LL BUG THE NEIGHBOR AGAIN IN THE MORNING.

LIKE I SAID, I'LL BE AWAY THIS WEEKEND.

SHE'LL *HAVE* TO SPIT IT OUT BY THEN...

I DIDN'T FIND YOUR PARENTS IN THE PHONEBOOK...
I'M AFRAID IF I DON'T HAVE MORE INFO, I'LL HAVE TO TAKE YOU TO THE POLICE.

...

8:30 PM
05/18/2013

DI
RS
demain
THURSDAY MARCH 12TH

DIARY 94-95

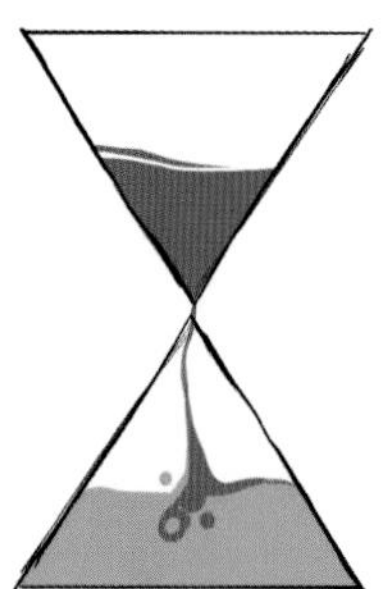

MAY 1995...
ARE YOU ALMOST DONE? WE STILL HAVE TO DO GEOGRAPHY AND MATH AFTER THIS...!
I'VE JUST GOT THREE POSES LEFT TO SHOOT ...AND THEN I HAVE TO GO. I'VE GOT LOTS TO DO TOO.

MOVE A LITTLE TO THE RIGHT, PLEASE...
THE BACKLIGHTING ISN'T SO BAD...

LIKE THIS?
PERFECT!

NOW LOOK AT ME...

LOWER YOUR SHOULDERS!

D'YA HAVE A STICK UP YOUR ASS OR WHAT?
BUT I... NO...!

HEY! I'M TRYING! YOU DON'T HAVE TO BE SO BOSSY!
I JUST WANT YOU TO LOOK YOUR BEST... YOU HAVE A PRETTY NECK. I WANT TO SHOW IT.

DON'T MOVE. I'LL SHOW YOU...

...
BACK UP A LITTLE BIT MORE...

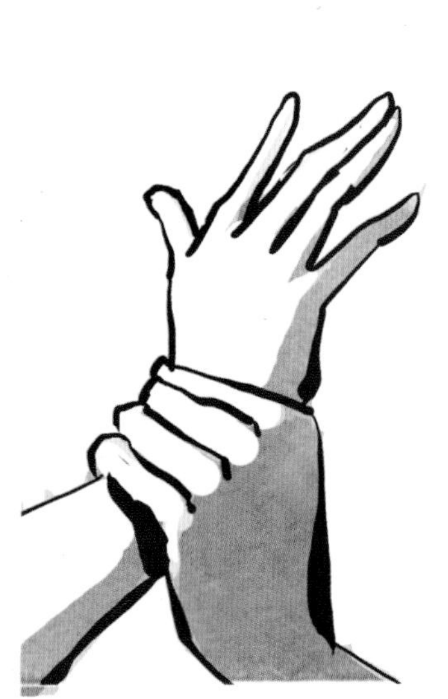

...

diohead
PABLO HONEY
NIRVANA
Patti Smith

radiohead
Patti Smith Group

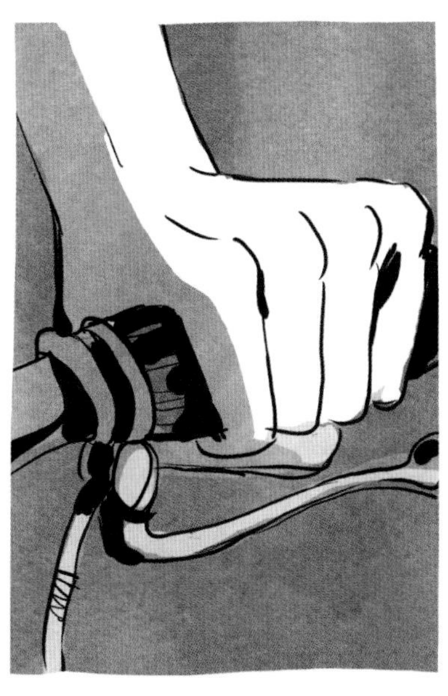
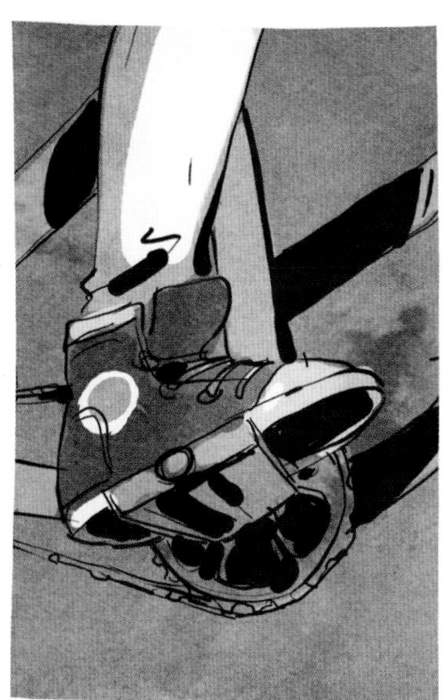

LUISA! IT'S *ABOUT TIME!*
SORRY, I HAD TO WORK.
MAN, YOU'RE A *PAIN*. WE'RE GOING TO MISS THE 5 O'CLOCK SHOW!

OOH! LOOK AT THE LEECH!

LUISA, YOU FORGOT YOUR CAMERA!

HEY, DYKE! WE DIDN'T INVITE *YOU!*

WHO'RE THESE *MORONS?!*
IT'S OKAY... DROP IT...
HEY, LUISA! LOOKS LIKE THE CARPET MUNCHER'S *CRUSHING* ON YOU. WATCH OUT OR YOU'LL CATCH HER DISEASE.

SHUT UP, YOU ASSHOLE!

YOU LEFTY EARLY SO YOU COULD HANG OUT WITH *THEM*?
SERIOUSLY, LUISA?

...
THE HELL! HAVEN'T YOU DATED A *REAL* GUY?!
YOU JUST HAVEN'T BEEN FUCKED RIGHT, *HUH?!*

LEAVE HER *ALONE*, OLIVER...
PFFFFT
SHE'S JUST LEAVING. GOING HOME TO *MOMMY & DADDY*.

WE'LL LEAVE WITH THE *REAL CHICKS*.

WE DON'T NEED TO PUT UP WITH *LOSERS!*

GO ON HOME
AND EAT SOME PUSSY,
BLONDIE!
ENOUGH, OLIVER, LEAVE HER ALONE. SHE'S GONE NOW...

BUT, SERIOUSLY, LOOK AT HER!

WITH HER CRAPPY LITTLE MOPED...
AW MAN! LOOK AT THE TIME!

WE TOTALLY MISSED THE MOVIE.

ALRIGHT! I'M COMING!

YEAH?!
SORRY. IT'S ME AGAIN. SASHA, YOUR NEIGHBOR.

DID THE KID GO HOME?
NO, ACTUALLY!

LISTEN... I THINK SHE RAN AWAY...OR SOMETHING...
LAST NIGHT, I LOOKED AT HER ID.

...IT *EXPIRED* OVER 10 YEARS AGO...
SO?!

SO SUPPOSEDLY SHE WAS BORN IN 1980...

SHE MUST HAVE STOLEN THE ID TO BUY SMOKES OR SOMETHING.
YOU SURE YOU DON'T KNOW HER?

SHE'S GOT NOWHERE TO GO. SHE'S *LOST*...

I DON'T WANT TO SAY SO BUT...
BUT *WHAT?!*

WELL...SHE LOOKS LIKE YOU. IT'S *OBVIOUS*.

YOU NEED TO FIND OUT WHAT HER DEAL IS. I DON'T THINK IT'S AN *ACCIDENT* SHE CAME HERE. I'M PRETTY POSITIVE...
...SHE ISN'T TELLING ME EVERYTHING.

BUT MAYBE TO YOU...

SO COULD I...
I HAD SOMETHING PLANNED THIS WEEKEND AND...

OH, HELL, NO!
SO NOW I GET TO SUFFER THE CONSEQUENCES OF *YOUR* GENEROSITY?

JUST FOR TWO DAYS. TO SEE! AFTER, WE'LL TAKE HER TO THE COPS IF SHE HASN'T EXPLAINED EVERYTHING.
YEAH... WELL, I MIGHT NOT WANT TO WAIT FOR YOU TO DO THAT...

YAY! THANK YOU!
YEAH YEAH. OKAY.

LUISA! GET YOUR BUTT OVER HERE!

LUISA?

COME HERE!
IT'LL BE GOOD FOR YOU TO TALK TO THE WOMAN WHO'S LIVING IN YOUR *APPARENTLY* DEAD AUNT'S APARTMENT...

I'LL WRITE DOWN YOUR NUMBER AND GIVE YOU MINE...
WHAT'S YOUR FIRST NAME AGAIN?

06 84 77 98 69 "LUISA."

OH. UH. NO...
I MEANT *YOUR* FIRST NAME IS...?

LUISA!
MY NAME'S LUISA TOO, DAMMIT!
WOW!

CRAZY!

...

NOW...
...YOU AND I HAVE SOME THINGS TO TALK ABOUT, I THINK...

I'LL LEAVE YOU TO IT, THEN...
LUISA, IF ANY PROBLEMS, DON'T HESITATE TO USE YOUR PHONE CARD, OKAY?

ARE YOU PUTTING ME ON?
YOU NEVER KNOW...

SHIT... THIS MUST BE A DREAM...
OKAY SO... IS IT REALLY 2013?! I SAW THE DATE ON SASHA'S COMPUTER...

HOW'S THAT POSSIBLE? THE DAY BEFORE YESTERDAY WAS 1995!

YOU'RE MESSING WITH ME!

NO!
I SWEAR!

OKAY! SO LET'S START AT THE BEGINNING: WHAT'S YOUR REAL NAME?
WHERE DO YOU KNOW MY AUNT FROM?

SO, WE'RE REALLY IN AURELIA'S APARTMENT?

YES! THAT WAS MY AUNT'S NAME. THIS IS THE APARTMENT SHE LEFT ME WHEN SHE DIED.
IF SHE WAS YOUR AUNT, TOO, YOU WOULD ALSO KNOW THAT SHE'S NO LONGER...

ACTUALLY, I DIDN'T KNOW...

IT'S BEEN TEN YEARS SINCE I LAST SAW HER...
MOM HASN'T SPOKEN TO HER IN A LONG TIME. SO...

OKAY...COULD YOU TELL ME YOUR MOTHER'S NAME, PLEASE?

JOELLE... JOELLE ARAMBOL-FOURNIER...

HEE HEE...YOURS, TOO?

YOUR ID, NOW!
SHOW ME YOUR PAPERS!

HEEEY!

2 SUPER POSTERS
10 AUTOCOLLANTS
DIARY
94-95
CARTE NATIONALE D'IDENTITÉ

NOM: ARAMBOL
ms: Luisa,Sophie
24 avril 1980
es (28)
É FRANÇAISE
. 62

CAN WE GO GRAB SOMETHING TO EAT?

I'M *STARVING.*

R
en Rocket

ART
Sandw
Grecs - Paninis - Tex
THERE'S A GYRO PLACE...CAN WE HAVE GYROS?
NO!

HURRY UP, NOW. YOU AND YOUR *HOOP* EARRINGS...

I ATE *ENOUGH* SHIT LIKE THAT WHEN I WAS YOUR AGE...

DO YOU *ALWAYS* CURSE EVERY OTHER WORD?
OH SHUT UP.

AT LEAST TIL WE GET TO THE SUSHI PLACE...
"SUSHI"?

YES, SUSHI. JAPANESE FOOD. ARE YOU GOING TO REPEAT EVERYTHING I SAY?
...
MENUS

WE'RE GOING TO EAT LIVE OCTOPUS AND STUFF?

...

ARE YOU A TOTAL IDIOT? OR ARE YOU LIKE THIS ON PURPOSE?

I DON'T KNOW THIS TYPE OF FOOD!

ISN'T THERE A CREPE STAND INSTEAD?
NO!

YOU'RE GOING TO TRY SUSHI AND...
I DIDN'T KNOW WHAT IT WAS WHEN I WAS 15 EITHER.

SUSHIS-YAKITORIS
Beauty La
SALON DE BEAU
YOU'LL BE AHEAD OF THE GIRLS YOUR AGE!
IT'LL GIVE YOU SOMETHING TO TALK TO YOUR FRIENDS ABOUT...

LET'S SIT OVER THERE...

WELL THIS IS TOTALLY AWESOME...
I'M IN 2013 AND I'M GOING TO EAT SUSHI...

ONE ON ONE WITH MY OLDER SPITTING IMAGE...
STOP TALKING *NONSENSE*...

HOW OLD'RE YOU?

MIND YOUR BUSINESS, ALRIGHT?

OKAY... I'M 33!

OH, YEAH? NO KIDDING? HOLY COW!
IT'S FINE. IT'S NOT THE END OF THE WORLD!

YOU LIVE ALONE?
YES!
WHY DO YOU GIVE A RAT'S ASS? YOU'RE LIKE MY MOTHER WITH YOUR STUPID QUESTIONS!

ALL TEENAGERS THINK ABOUT IS HOOKING UP. IT'S *OBSESSIVE*!

33 YEARS OLD AND *NO* BF...? HOW'S THAT *POSSIBLE?*

ONE DAY, YOU FALL ASLEEP SINGLE AT AGE 15...
AND *POOF,* YOU WAKE UP 17 YEARS LATER...

AND THERE'S STILL NOBODY...
THAT'S HOW IT'S POSSIBLE...

HEY! LET ME SEE THAT!?
...

YOU'D HAVE TO *PAY* TEENS TO WEAR THAT TODAY!

THIS IS SO *CRAZY!*
I'VE GOT TWO MORE AT HOME. LUCY GAVE THEM TO ME.

I KNOW...
BUT...THAT'S IMPOSSIBLE ...

I'M *YOU* AND YOU'RE *ME?!*
YES!

COME TO THINK OF IT, I REALLY *DID* HAVE A CRAPPY, OLD STYLE LIKE THAT...
AH, YOU SEE!

I'M SURE THAT'S IT! YOU'RE THE FUTURE ME!
YOU'RE MY OLDER DOUBLE!
THAT'S SO *WICKED!*

EXCUSE ME, HELLO!
HAVE YOU DECIDED YET?

...

YEP... OKAY...

WE'LL HAVE TWO BENTO BOXES, PLEASE!
OKAY!

HA! HA! IT'S FUNNY!
YOU TWO LOOK LIKE SISTERS...

YES! LIKE TWIN SISTERS–17 YEARS APART!
WE GET IT, THANK YOU!

YEAH!
THE SAME MUG BUT WITH MORE WRINKLES!

GAH! SHUT THE HELL UP NOOOW!

...

SO, LET'S CONCEDE...

LET'S CONCEDE THAT WE ARE IN A CRAZY SCI-FI WORLD AND YOU'RE REALLY ME...

WHAT I WANT TO UNDERSTAND...

IS *WHY*, AND *HOW* YOU TURNED UP HERE...

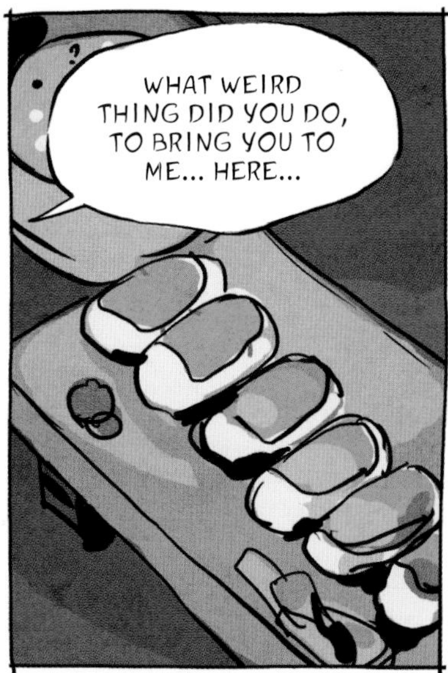
WHAT WEIRD THING DID YOU DO, TO BRING YOU TO ME... HERE...

HEY, I HAVE NO IDEA!
I WENT TO SEE AGNES... I TOOK A BUS TO GO HOME...

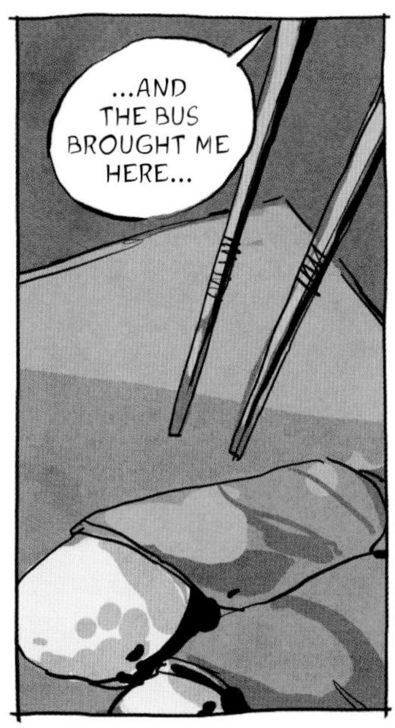
...AND THE BUS BROUGHT ME HERE...

SO MAYBE *YOU* DID SOMETHING STUPID!

OKAY...
SOME SILVERWARE FOR THE YOUNG LADY, PLEASE!

DO YOU THINK YOU COULD LEND ME YOUR PHONE?
TO DO WHAT?
SO I CAN CALL MOM...

AND TELL HER WHAT?
"HI, MOM! IT'S LUISA. I'M A BIT LATE. I TOOK A LITTLE TRIP TO MY FUTURE, I'LL BE BACK HOME SOON..."

WHY DOESN'T HER NUMBER WORK ANYMORE?
SHE...
SHE ISN'T *DEAD*, IS SHE?

NO, SHE MOVED TO BE CLOSER TO ME...

EXCEPT WE ONLY SEE EACH OTHER EVERY SIX MONTHS...

WHICH IS LESS THAN BEFORE...

EVERY TIME WE GET TOGETHER, I GET THE SAME QUESTIONS...THE SAME ONES YOU WERE ASKING...
"YOU STILL DON'T HAVE A BOYFRIEND? WHAT'RE YOU WAITING FOR TO GET MARRIED?"

ANYWAY, IT BUGS ME.
IT SMOTHERS ME. SHE'S ALWAYS BEEN SMOTHERING.

EVEN AT *YOUR* AGE, I WASN'T ALLOWED TO DO THIS OR SEE THAT PERSON...
NOTHING'S CHANGED! IT WEARS ME OUT.

SO, WE GO TO THE MUSEUM TWICE A YEAR, WE TALK ABOUT WEATHER AND STUFF, AND THAT'S ENOUGH... WE'RE DONE.

...

MAYBE SHE'S JUST WORRIED.
...I AM, TOO...

WHEN I SEE HOW...
HOW WHAT?!

HOW I LIVE? WHAT YOUR LIFE WILL LOOK LIKE IN 17 YEARS?
THANKS A LOT!
KEEP IT UP AND I'LL WALK OUT AND LEAVE YOU WITH THE CHECK!

AND YOU'LL BE TOTALLY SCREWED, WITH YOUR WORTHLESS CASH!

I'M ALREADY SCREWED...
SO AM I!

I JUST REMEMBERED I HAD PLANS TONIGHT!
GAH! THIS SUCKS!

JUST LEAVE ME. I'LL TAKE CARE OF MYSELF...
NO WAY!

YOU'RE COMING WITH ME!
BUT, FIRST, YOU'RE GETTING A NEW T-SHIRT.

BECAUSE I CAN'T STAND THE SMELL OF ROAD KILL ANY MORE...

WHAT?!
...

I'LL BUY IT FOR YOU...
AND YOU'LL AUTO-REIMBURSE ME WHEN YOU'RE OLDER...

SUSHIS / YAKITORI
MENUS
I'M GOING NUTS...

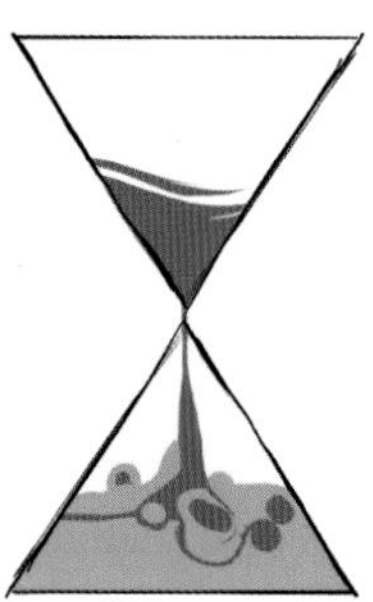

-20%
SO...

DON'T YOU FIND YOUR APARTMENT A LITTLE *SMALL?*
ARE YOU KIDDING?

THAT TWO-ROOM APARTMENT IS A *GODSEND!*
DO YOU KNOW WHAT RENTS ARE LIKE IN PARIS?
WOW, YOU'RE A PAIN IN THE ASS! UNBELIEVABLE!

PUT THAT DOWN, PLEASE!

WE'RE SEEING SOME FRIENDS TONIGHT...
WE'RE NOT GOING *LAP DANCING!*

THANK YOU!

I DIDN'T KNOW AUNTIE AURELIA LIVED IN SUCH A TINY APARTMENT!
DO YOU KNOW WHAT SHE DIED OF?
SOLDES
NOT REALLY... HEART ATTACK, I THINK..

SOLDES
SHE LIVED ALONE. NOBODY'D HEARD FROM HER.

I SWEAR I DON'T KNOW WHY SHE PUT ME IN HER WILL...

I HADN'T SEEN HER SINCE I...*WE* WERE FIVE.
FOREVER Bitch
MOM ALWAYS AVOIDED THE "*AURELIA*" TOPIC.

PUT THAT DOWN, PLEASE!
FOREVER Bitch

HONESTLY! COULD YOU FIND ANYTHING *CRUDER*?

WHAT DO WE DO ABOUT SASHA?
WE CAN'T TELL HER THE *TRUTH!*

AND I DON'T WANT TO BE TAKEN TO THE COPS!

WE'LL FIGURE OUT SOMETHING...
...'CAUSE IF WE EXPLAIN WHAT WE SEEM TO UNDERSTAND ABOUT THE SITUATION TO HER, THEN...

...WE COULD *BOTH* END UP BEING TAKEN TO THE COPS!

MAYBE WE'D EVEN EARN OURSELVES AN INVITATION FOR TWO AT BEDLAM...

"BEDLAM?"

...
SHE TIRES ME OUT...

HEEEYOOO!
SASHA?

CAN YOU PASS ME THE WATER BOTTLE, PLEASE?
SURE...

JUST GIVE ME A SEC.

HERE YOU GO...

THANKS!

GORGEOUS, ISN'T IT?

HEY...ARE YOU GIVING ME THE SILENT TREATMENT?

HUH?!
UH...*NO!* I HAVE A LOT ON MY MIND...

I WAS HELPING OUT A LOST KID RIGHT BEFORE I LEFT...
A NEIGHBOR'S TAKING CARE OF HER NOW.
I SEE...

YOU WANTED TO ADOPT HER?
TCH!

BUT NOW... YOU'RE SHARING CUSTODY OF HER WITH YOUR NEIGHBOR?!
HATS OFF!

MADAME'S GOING FASTER THAN *EVERYONE* ELSE!

...

ALRIGHTY!

VRRRRRR

VRRRRRRR

TIP

Luisa Neighbor
HI!
THE KID'S A COUSIN
I'D NEVER MET. SHE RAN
AWAY. WE'RE GETTING TO
KNOW EACH OTHER. ;-).
ALL'S GOING WELL.
YOUR NEIGHBOR.

WELL, WELL...

SHIT SASHA, COME ON!

ARE YOU WAITING FOR *NOAH'S ARK* OR SOMETHING?
SERIOUSLY, JUST UNPLUG FROM PARIS FOR *TWO MINUTES?!*

MAN, YOU SUCK!
OKAY, OKAY! I'M COMING!

MAY, 1995

WHAT HAPPENED WITH LUCY? YOU GUYS AREN'T TALKING NOW?

OH UM... SUNDAY, I SPENT THE AFTERNOON WITH HER GOING OVER THE PLAY. AND SHE TRIED TO FOLLOW ME WHEN I MET UP WITH FANNY AND SOME OTHER KIDS TO GO TO THE MOVIES.

BUT SHE WASN'T INVITED, YOU KNOW... THAT'S ALL. IT WAS JUST A WEIRD THING.

AND NOW, SHE'S STOPPED TALKING TO ME...
THAT'S TOO MUCH... YOU DON'T JUST *INVITE* YOURSELF!
ESPECIALLY SINCE FANNY'S COUSINS CAN'T STAND HER.

DON'T YOU THINK LUCY CLINGS TO YOU A LITTLE TOO MUCH?
YAH. IT'S A LITTLE ANNOYING.

ESPECIALLY SINCE MY MOM DOESN'T WANT ME TO TALK TO HER. SHE THINKS SHE'S TOO "PROVOCATIVE"...

WELL, OBVIOUSLY WHEN YOU'RE DIFFERENT LIKE THAT, YOU CAN AT LEAST *TRY* NOT TO GET YOURSELF NOTICED.
IF I WAS HER, I WOULDN'T TRY STANDING OUT SO MUCH AT SCHOOL, YOU KNOW.

WITH EVERYTHING THEY SAY ABOUT HER...
SERIOUSLY!

SHE HASN'T TRIED TO *HIT* ON YOU, HAS SHE?
NO WAY! SHE KNOWS I'M NOT LIKE THAT!

HMMM
...

PFFF... WHATEVER!
OKAY... OKAY...

ACTUALLY, I'VE BEEN WONDERING ABOUT SOMETHING...

WHY *DO* YOU FALL FOR ONE PERSON INSTEAD OF ANOTHER?
UHM...IT'S NOT REALLY A QUESTION OF CHOICE. IT'S FATE...

YEAH. I HOPE I'LL FIND MY SOULMATE SOME DAY!
WELL, TURN OVER YOUR CARDS TO SEE!

WHAT'S THIS ONE?
OH, THAT. GENERALLY, IT MEANS CHANGE.

ARE YOU SHITTING ME? THAT'S *DEATH!*
YEEEAH. BUT THAT DOESN'T NECESSARILY SUCK.

AND THE CARD NEXT TO IT?
IT'S THE LOVERS CARD. IT MEANS YOU'LL HAVE TO MAKE SOME *CHOICES.*
LIKE EVERYONE, YOU KNOW...

AND YOU *BELIEVE* THIS CRAP?
MY MOTHER GOES TO A PSYCHIC EVERY YEAR...

SHE'S THE ONE WHO TAUGHT ME TO READ TAROT. SHE SAID I'D FIND THE MAN OF MY LIFE IN THREE YEARS.

LIKE, WE'LL HAVE *KIDS* TOGETHER AND *EVERYTHING!*
PFF! SO SHE MOSTLY SAW HOW *GULLIBLE* YOU ARE!

HEY, IT'S NO JOKE. SHE FORESAW MY AUNT'S SHINGLES!
AND THE DEATH OF OUR CAT, TORPEDO!

GAH! I KNOW WHAT THE DEATH CARD MEANS!

I'M LATE AND MY MOTHER'S GOING TO *KILL* ME!

I GOTTA GO, AGNES!
OKAY! SEE YOU MONDAY!

I'LL BRING THE CARDS. WE CAN FINISH AT SCHOOL!
YEAH, KNOW WHAT? I DON'T THINK IT WILL CHANGE ANYTHING IN MY LIFE!

CLACK

HELLO! EXCUSE ME, ARE YOU GOING TO COUDRAY?
I'M DONE WITH MY SHIFT, BUT IT'S ON THE WAY...
OH...

AH, COME ON.

THANKS! HERE'S MY SCHOOL ID!
OKAY, OKAY!

THAT'LL DO...

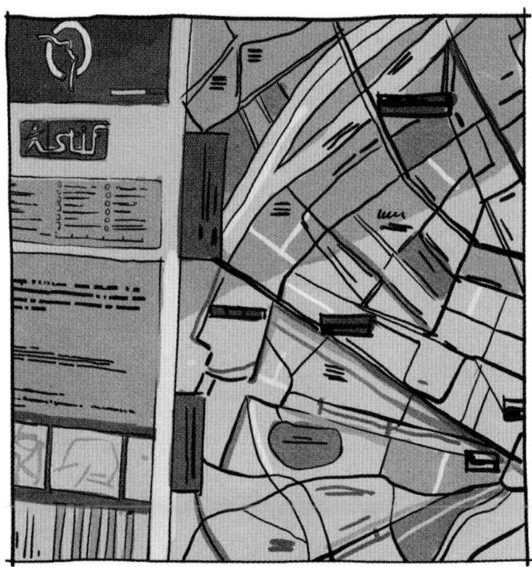

WHAT EXACTLY ARE YOU DOING NOW?

WE'RE GOING TO BE LATE...

I'M LOOKING AT THE BUS LINES... TO GET BACK HOME...
LOOK FOR A TELEPORTATION BOOTH. IT'LL BE QUICKER...

SERIOUSLY?! THEY INVENTED TELEPORTATION?
OH, COME ON...

THAT DOESN'T EXIST!

AND I DON'T THINK THE BUS WILL BE THE EASIEST WAY FOR YOU TO GET HOME...

...

YOU'RE CRYING?

CRAP...SHE'S CRYING...

I'M *SICK* OF THIS!
YEAH, ME, TOO. I THOUGHT THAT IN 2013, CARS WOULD BE ABLE TO FLY...AND NOPE, THEY DON'T...

WHEN I'M 33 YEARS OLD, I'LL STILL BE *SINGLE*!!
OH MY GOD, SHUT UP!

YOU KNOW OUR FRIEND, AGNES? I'M NOT JUDGING GIRLS LIKE THAT... BUT THERE'RE LOTS OF CHICKS YOU KNOW, LIKE AGNES, WHO ARE MOTHERS TWO TIMES OVER BY TIME THEY'RE 25. WHEN *I WAS* 25 I'D JUST FINISHED SCHOOL. EVERYONE GOES AT THEIR OWN PACE, OKAY? THAT'S ALL!
WHAT?!

LOOK, IT'LL BE FINE!

WE NEED TO PICK UP THE PACE! YOU'LL SEE WHAT BECAME OF AGNES!

I'M SCARED...

JUST REMEMBER WHAT WE SAID, OKAY?

RIGHT... I'M A DISTANT COUSIN WHO RAN AWAY... I ACT LIKE I DON'T KNOW HER...

RIGHT! AND YOU LET ME LEAD THE CONVERSATION!

IT'S TOO BAD SOPHIE AND AMBER ARE WITH THEIR FATHER TONIGHT; SHE'D BE LESS BORED...

SO, THEN, IS WHAT MY COUSIN SAID TRUE...
YOU HAVE KIDS?

YES, THEY'RE A LITTLE *YOUNGER* THAN YOU, BUT YES...
SOPHIE STARTS SEVENTH GRADE NEXT YEAR. I *STILL* CAN'T BELIEVE IT.

HOLY COW! TIME FLIES!
WHAT CAN I GET YOU?

DO YOU HAVE FRUIT JUICE FOR THE KID?

YOU'RE *KIDDING*, RIGHT?
YOU WANT US TO PUT ON A *RAFFI* ALBUM IN THE BACKGROUND WHILE WE'RE AT IT?

NO, BUT I THINK THE YOUNG LADY'LL HAVE A LITTLE MOJITO!
REALLY? CAN I?

GO ON!
ONE WON'T
HURT!
THANKS!
GO
EASY!
THAT'LL BE A
CHANGE FOR YOU
FROM A VIRGIN
COLADA, HA HA HA!

WHEN I THINK BACK,
WE USED TO DRINK
ALL THOSE BAR
DRINKS...
RUM AND COKE,
STUFF LIKE THAT...LUCKILY
OUR TASTE'S MORE
REFINED NOW...

I'LL GO GET
SOME BEERS...

JULIA *STILL* ILLUSTRATES
WHAT SHE SAYS BY DOING
THE OPPOSITE...
I LIKE
HER THAT
WAY...

SO ANYWAY,
DO YOU STILL
READ TAROT?
SORRY?

YESSS! HAHA!
I TOLD HER ABOUT THE TIME YOU READ MY CARDS! DO YOU REMEMBER?

AGNES? YOU WERE INTO THAT *SILLINESS?*
I DIDN'T KNOW ABOUT YOUR "*WOOWOO*" SIDE!

HONESTLY, I JUST READ TAROT FOR *FUN*...
YOU KNOW, WE ALL GO THROUGH AN MYSTIC PHASE WHEN WE'RE *KIDS*...THEN IT PASSES...

LUISA, WHAT *ELSE* DID YOU TELL YOUR COUSIN?
OH I KNOW!

SHE TOLD HER THAT YOU'RE BETTER AT SEEING THE PAST IN A BRANDY SNIFTER THAN THE FUTURE IN A CRYSTAL BALL! HAHAHA!
TCH!

YEAH BUT, THE CARDS TOLD THE TRUTH ABOUT *YOUR* FUTURE...
A HUSBAND, TWO KIDS, ALL PRETTY QUICKLY...

BUT THEY *DIDN'T* SEE YOU'D GET DIVORCED JUST AS FAST!
THAT'S *TOO* BAD...

BUT, ARE YOU HAPPY? WHAT DO YOU DO FOR A LIVING?
I'M A NURSE'S AIDE...IT SUITS ME *VERY* WELL, THANK YOU!

GIVE YOUR COUSIN ANOTHER DRINK. SHE'S FREAKING ME OUT!
...

EITHER SHE DRINKS OR WE CALL AN EXORCIST!

BUT ISN'T THAT A *WASTE?*
YOU WANTED TO BE A *SURGEON!*
HEY, OOOH!

THAT'S *ENOUGH!*
THAT'S ENOUGH! PUT A *LID* ON IT!

NO, LET HER TALK...
SHE'S NOT COMPLETELY WRONG.

I WANTED TO GO TOO FAST. I WAS SO PROUD WHEN I GOT HITCHED RIGHT OUT OF SCHOOL.
AND THEN LIFE JUST ATE AWAY AT MY AMBITION...

BUT IF YOU SAY "WASTE" AGAIN TALKING ABOUT MY JOB, MY LIFE, OR MY KIDS, I'LL HOOK YOUR EARRINGS ONTO YOUR SCRUNCHIE AND MAKE YOU EAT THEM TO WASH DOWN ALL THAT JUDGING!

UNDERSTOOD!?

AND YOU NEED TO BE MORE DISCREET!
WHAT?!

CLEARLY YOU MUST HAVE TOLD HER STUFF ABOUT ME, OR SHE WOULDN'T BE DOING THIS PSYCHIC ROUTINE ON ME.

IT'S LIKE THAT WITH YOUNG PEOPLE. THEIR AMBITIONS ARE BIGGER THAN THEIR ABILITIES.

LIKE, OKAY, KID...WHAT DO YOU WANT TO BE WHEN YOU'RE OLDER?
A FINE ART PHOTOGRAPHER, WHY?

WELL, YOUR COUSIN CAN SAY A THING OR TWO ABOUT THAT! HAHA!

SHE WANTED THE SAME THING WHEN SHE WAS YOUR AGE!
WHAT DOES THAT MEAN? "WANTED"?
...

LOOK, I'M DEFINITELY A PHOTOGRAPHER...I JUST HAD TO MAKE SOME *COMPROMISES* SO I COULD EAT...
THAT'S ALL...

SHE TAKES PORNO PICTURES! HAHAHAHA!

HEY, QUIT TALKING NONSENSE!

DON'T LISTEN TO HER. IT'S NOT LIKE THAT.
BWAHHHHH...

GAH! SHE'S JUST A KID! HOW ABOUT YOU GET YOURSELF TOGETHER?

OH, YOUR COUSIN UNDERVALUES HER WORK. I THINK IT'S SEXY, TAKING PICTURES OF HAM...
OF HAM... OF WHAT?
GOD YOU'RE A PAIN IN THE ASS...

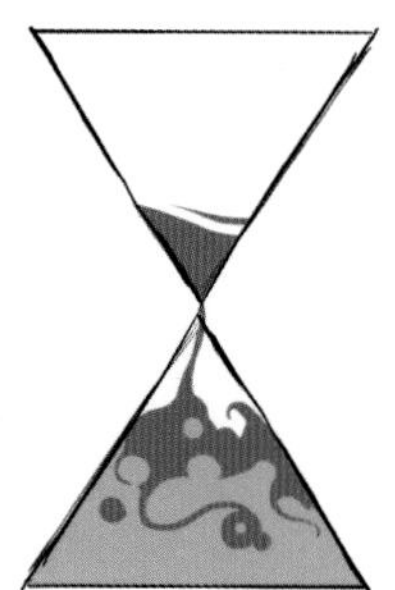

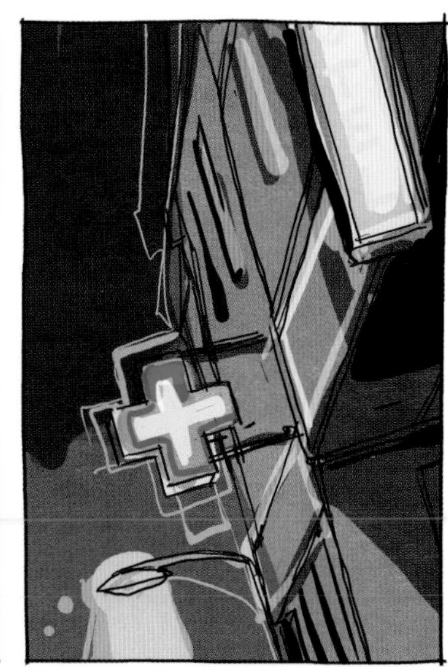

COME ON!

YOU HAD *TWO* DRINKS. THAT'S NOT ENOUGH TO TURN YOUR STOMACH!

IT'S NOT JUST MY STOMACH...
I'M BUMMED...

YOU OBVIOUSLY DIDN'T STAY IN TOUCH WITH LUCY!
WHAT?

WHICH LUCY? WOW ALCOHOL AFFECTS KIDS QUICKLY!
BWAHHHHH...

ANYWAY, YOU WEREN'T EXACTLY SUBTLE TONIGHT...
I ALMOST HAD TO HAVE IT OUT FOR REAL WITH AGNES...

GAH! I TOLD YOU TO STAY QUIET!
BWAHHHHH...
HEEERE WE GO GAIN!

IT'S STRONGER THAN ME. I CAN'T HELP IT!
YES YOU CAN!

YOU CAN KEEP YOUR MOUTH SHUT!
YOU'RE COMPLETELY PHYSICALLY CAPABLE OF DOING THAT!

BUT I WANT TO KNOW THINGS!

THERE'S NO POINT TURNING YOUR BRAIN INSIDE OUT WITH STUFF ABOUT THE FUTURE.

COME ON. WE'RE GOING HOME!

...

WHAT THE HELL?!

YOU'RE...YOU'RE DISINTEGRATING?

GOD, I MUST BE DRUNKER THAN YOU ARE... ARE YOU OKAY?
I'LL-- I'LL BE OKAY, I THINK...

...BUT YOU **HAVE** TO GO BACK!

HOTEL

OH, MY GOD...WHAT'S THIS NOW?

I THOUGHT I WAS *DONE* WITH THIS CRAP...

PFFFFFFFF...

GODDAMN IT...

TAP

LUISA, IS THAT YOU?

YOU'RE *PUSHING* IT. I SAID 6 O'CLOCK! I'VE BEEN WORRIED SICK!

IT'S NOT MY FAULT! I DIDN'T NOTICE THE TIME!

WHY DIDN'T YOU CALL?
WHERE WERE YOU?

I TOLD YOU I WAS AT AGNES'.
WE TALKED ABOUT OUR FUTURES...

SURE. OR YOU WERE AT SOMEONE *ELSE'S* HOUSE. MAYBE SOME DAY YOU'LL STOP LYING TO ME...

I WASN'T AT LUCY'S, IF THAT'S WHAT YOU'RE THINKING...

I HOPE YOU'RE NOT LYING. YOU KNOW I DON'T WANT YOU TO SEE HER...

TELL ME WHY.

WE'LL TALK ABOUT IT LATER...
EAT YOUR DINNER, IT'S GETTING COLD.

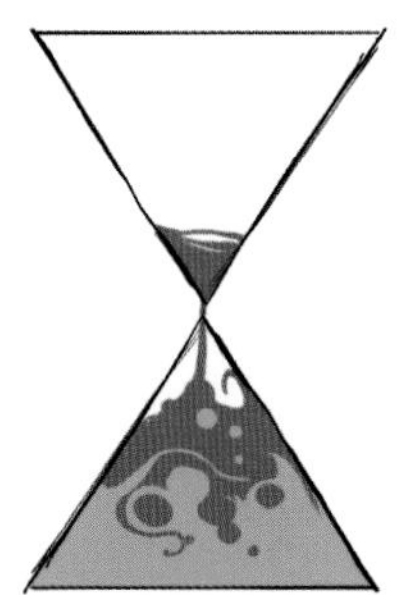

CLICK
CLICK
CLICK

CLICK
CLICK
CLICK

CLICK
CLICK

?

RIIIIIIIIIIIING

YES! COMING!

MS. ARAMBOL?
IT'S ME, YOUR NEIGH...

YEAH?

YOU CAN CALL ME LUISA, TOO...
IT'S ALLOWED, YOU KNOW...

RIGHT. LUISA... SO HOW'S IT GOING?

HOW'S THE GIRL?

UH... WELL...SHE'S FINE...
ACTUALLY, SHE'S ZONKED OUT. SHE'S FEELING A LITTLE SICK...

SICK?
YES...JUST TIRED... NOTHING SERIOUS. I'LL KEEP HER AT MY PLACE WHILE SHE MAKES UP HER MIND ABOUT GOING BACK TO HER PARENTS...

OH GOOD! PERFECT.
BETTER IT ENDS THIS WAY THAN GOING DOWN TO THE POLICE STATION.

SO SHE *IS* A COUSIN OF YOURS?
A DISTANT COUSIN, YEAH. SHE FOUGHT WITH HER PARENTS AND RAN AWAY. TO HERE...

AND SINCE THREE-QUARTERS OF MY FAMILY AREN'T TALKING TO EACH OTHER, I DIDN'T KNOW HER.

YOU EVEN HAVE THE *SAME* NAME!
IT'S ONE OF OUR GREAT-GRAND-MOTHERS'...

WE LIKE PASSING DOWN FIRST NAMES IN OUR FAMILY...
INDEED...

THERE, YOU KNOW EVERYTHING...
I WON'T KEEP YOU...

OH! JUST ONE MORE THING!

SINCE TOMORROW'S A HOLIDAY, I'M HAVING A HOUSEWARMING PARTY TONIGHT.

I WANTED TO WARN YOU ABOUT THE NOISE...
AND INVITE YOU...

...

IT'S JUST... I HAVE A FRIEND, WHO'S SUPPOSED TO STOP BY...
AND THE KID'S WIPED OUT, SO...

OH, OKAY, TOO BAD...
I WOULD'VE LIKED TO SEE HER AGAIN...

I'LL TELL HER!
HAVE A NICE DAY!

UH... THANK...
SLAM

OKAY... SO WHERE WAS I?

RAAAAA!

LUISA?
ARE YOU OKAY?

AAAAAAARGHH

SERIOUSLY?

SINCE WHEN DO I HAVE *WHITE* HAIRS?

TROUBLE WAKING UP?
WANT SOME SODA TO SETTLE THE STOMACH?

WHAT WERE YOU DOING?
NOTHING...
DID YOU JUST GET UP?

OH, HEY!
WHERE'RE YOU GOING?

I'M GOING HOME.
IT'S ENOUGH. I'VE SEEN ENOUGH. I'M TAKING THE BUS BACK...

COME ON! YOU'RE TIRED... JUST WAIT A BIT.
WE'LL FIND YOUR SO-CALLED "MAGIC BUS" TOGETHER!

NO! I'M GOING ALONE!
YOU STAY IN *YOUR* WORLD!

MY "*WORLD*"?!
LOOK, MY OWN WORLD'S NO MORE *ROTTEN* THAN YOURS, KID!

BLAM!

MAN! WHAT A *BRAT*!

WELL... OKAY.
SHE GOT HERE ALONE, LIKE A GROWNUP...

SHE CAN LEAVE LIKE A GROWNUP...

56

YOU LOOK UPSET...
...

ACTUALLY YOU LOOK REALLY CRANKY...

RiiiiIiiiiNG

I'LL GET IT!
IT'S PROBABLY FOR YOUR NEIGHBOR!

WHATEVER! THANKS FOR THE COMPLIMENTS, YOU JERK!
HAHAHA!

HELLO! THE PARTY'S NOT HERE. IT'S OVER THERE ACROSS THE HALL...

EXCUSE ME, BUT...
WHO ARE YOU?

UH...

AH, WAIT A SECOND.
LET HER IN. IT'S MY COUSIN.

WHAT ON EARTH?
YOU DIDN'T LEAVE?
NO...MY BUS DIDN'T COME...
OBVIOUSLY...

GEEZ, LUISA, YOU COULD HELP HER OUT A LITTLE MORE THAN THAT...

YOU DON'T HAVE TO TAKE THE BUS. I CAN GIVE YOU MONEY FOR A TAXI...
DO YOUR PARENTS LIVE FAR?

WHO IS *HE*?! YOUR BOYFRIEND?

HAHAHAHA! THAT'S *ALL* I NEED!
THANKS *A LOT*!

IT *IS* WILD HOW MUCH YOUR COUSIN LOOKS LIKE YOU!

SHE'S LIKE A *PHOTOCOPY* OF YOU!

BUT "FRESHER"!
HEY!

I'M STARVING.

COOL! WE'VE GOT AT LEAST *ONE* THING IN COMMON!
SO. IS THE CRAZINESS ACROSS THE HALL GOING ON ALL NIGHT?

DON'T KNOW... THEY'RE OFF TO A GOOD START THOUGH...

HEY, THERE'RE NO *GUYS* OVER IN THERE...
QUIT FANTASIZING!

SERIOUSLY, YOU SHOULD COME SEE THIS!
LIKE, IT'S *TOTALLY* UNRESTRAINED!
WHICH ONE'S YOUR NEIGHBOR?
THE BLONDE...

OKAY, THERE'RE A LOT OF BLONDES THERE!

SHE MUST'VE *DROWNED* IN THAT TSUNAMI OF ESTROGEN!
TSSSSK...

I THINK MAYBE I'LL GO JOIN THEM...

HEY...
THAT'S HER AT THE WINDOW...

BUT... WHAT'S SHE...?

...

QUITE THE RASCAL, YOUR NEIGHBOR!
WHAT ARE YOU DOING?
WE'RE HAVING FUN!

SINCE YOU DON'T HAVE A TV!
...

YEAH, WELL, IT'S NOT POLITE TO *OGLE!*
SIT DOWN. LET'S EAT.

?!

DAMN, THAT WAS *HOT!*

I'M OVERHEATED. GIVE ME TWO ICE CUBES, PLEASE!

EVEN THE *KID* CAN'T BELIEVE HER EYES! HAHA!

HEY, LUISA. YOU ALRIGHT? IT'S NO BIG DEAL!
GET OVER IT.

BUT IT'S *OUTRAGEOUS!*

OUT OF CURIOSITY, WHEN YOU WAKE UP IN THE MORNING...
...YOU MAKE A PRACTICE OF ANOINTING YOURSELF WITH HOLY WATER?
FARID!

OKAY OKAY! I'M JUST SAYING, DON'T SAY IT'S "OUTRAGEOUS." IT'S NOT A BIG DEAL.

DOESN'T IT BOTHER YOU?
OF COURSE NOT... IT'S JUST THE WHOLE "VOYEUR OPEN BAR FOR ALL THE NEIGHBORS IN THE BUILDING TO STARE AT" THAT BUGS ME...

WOW LUISA, WHY IS THIS SHAKING *YOU* UP SO MUCH?
YOU KNOW, WE'RE ALL MORE OR LESS *BI*...

RIGHT. YOU'D LOVE THAT.
LOOK AT HER. SHE LOOKS LIKE SHE'S NEVER SEEN TWO *CHICKS MAKING OUT!*

PFFF...WELL THAT'S NOT TRUE...
OF COURSE SHE'S SEEN TWO GIRLS KISSING! SHE *KNOWS* ALL ABOUT IT.

NO I DON'T!

YES YOU DO!
WAIT. WHAT?

DON'T LIE TO YOURSELF, LUISA!
YOU KNOW DAMN WELL YOU CAN FEEL THINGS FOR GIRLS! YOU DON'T HAVE TO HIDE.

OKAY, MAYBE LET'S LEAVE THE KID ALONE...

THAT'S NOT TRUE!
I'M NOT LYING!

OF COURSE, YOU ARE! WHEN YOU'RE YOUNG, YOU SAY, IT'S NOTHING, "IT WILL PASS..."

THEN THERE'S OTHER PEOPLE'S JUDGMENTS, AND THEY EAT AWAY AT YOUR SELF ESTEEM...
IT ISN'T EASY TO ACCEPT THESE DESIRES.

...

LOOK IT JUST BUGS ME THAT SHE'S ACTING ALL *ALARMED* *ABOUT IT!*

IT'S FREAKIN' HYPOCRITICAL!

IS IT ME OR IS IT TOTALLY *WILD* HOW MUCH YOU LOOK LIKE EACH OTHER!?

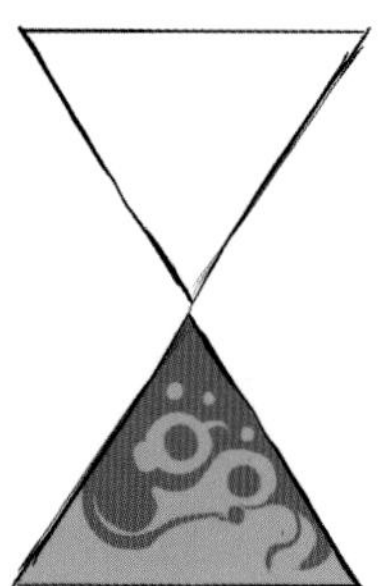

GROUIIIK.

GRROUU.

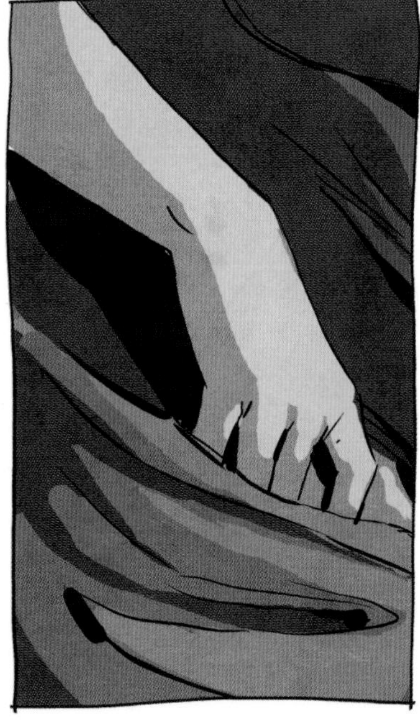

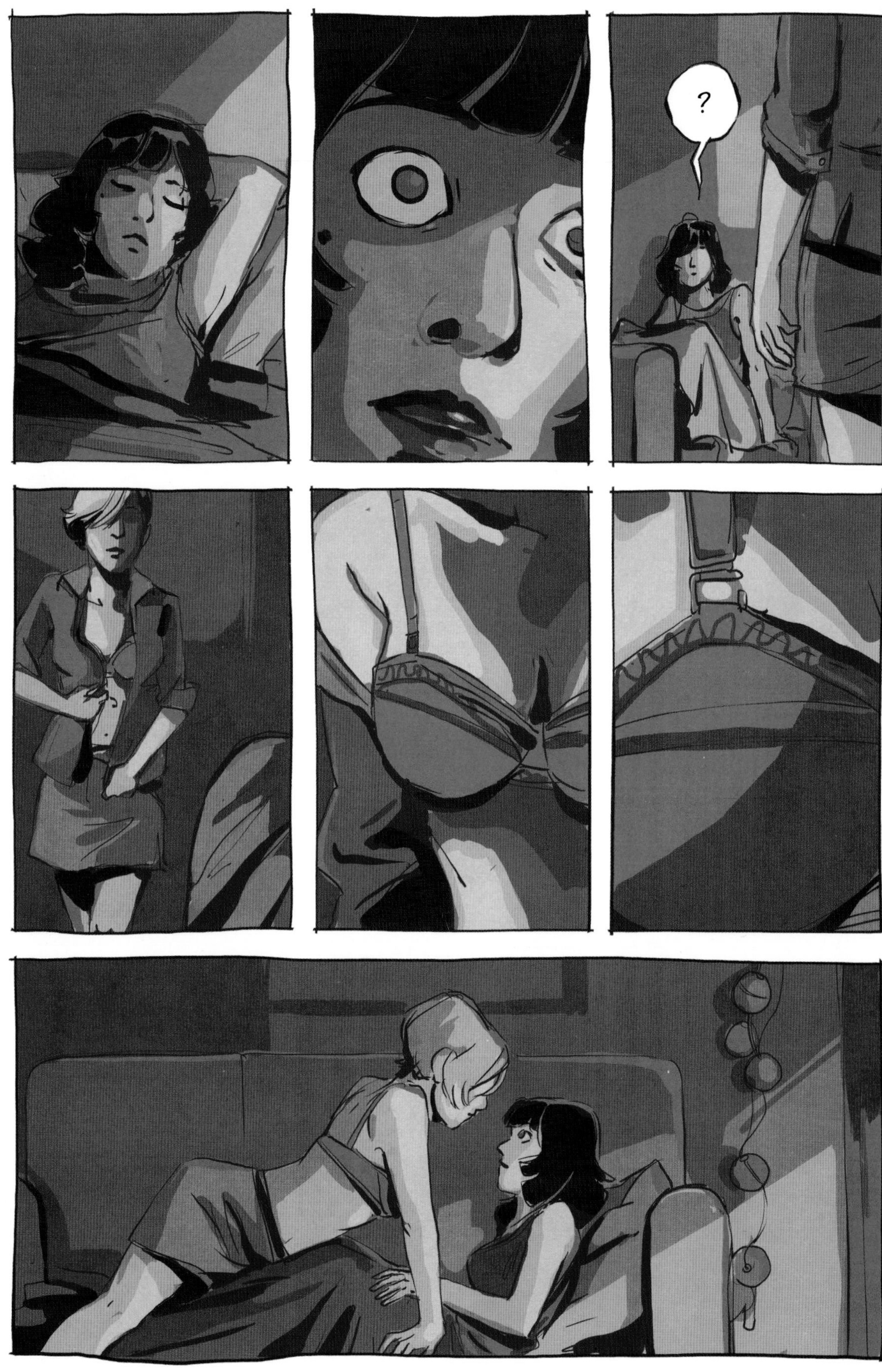

LUISA!
LUISA!

LUISA! WAKE UP! I'M WORRIED!

LUISA!
MMM... RELAX, THERE'S NOTHING TO WORRY ABOUT...

YES, THERE IS! SHOW ME YOUR HANDS!
MMMMPH...

IT'S 6 O'CLOCK IN THE MORNING. WHAT IS YOUR PROBLEM!?
YOUR HANDS!

...

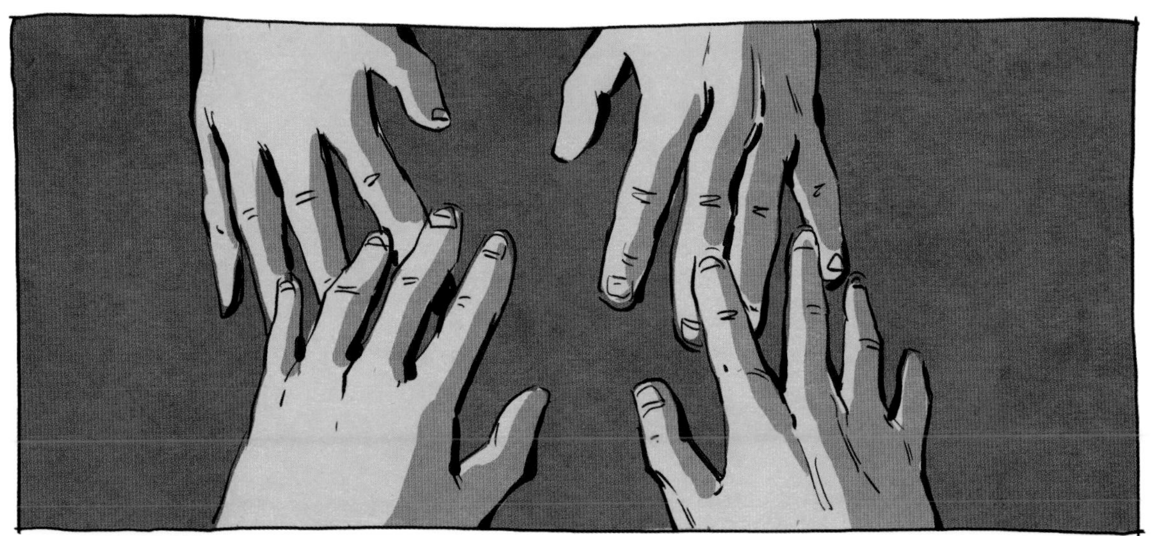

SHIT!
LOOK AT MINE!
ONE HAND LOOKS OLDER THAN THE OTHER!

THIS IS A *MESS!* WHAT THE HELL IS GOING ON?!

I DON'T KNOW... IT'S AS IF... WE'RE TURNING INTO EACH OTHER... *I'M* BECOMING YOU AND *YOU'RE* BECOMING ME.

YOU HAVE TO HELP ME GET BACK...
WE DON'T HAVE A CHOICE...

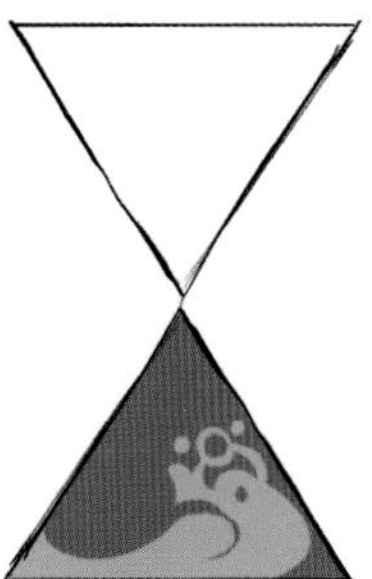

GYROS
YOU WANT LETTUCE, TOMATOES, AND ONIONS WITH THAT?

Kebob&Co
YES, PLEASE... I DON'T KNOW ABOUT HER, BUT I'M STARVING.

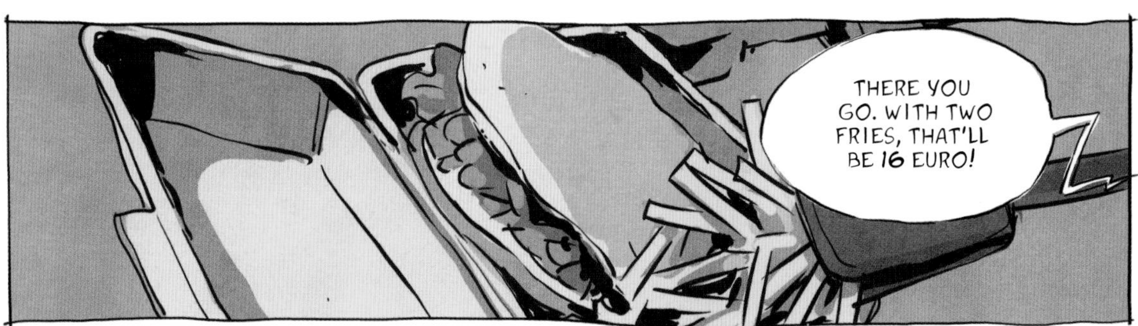
THERE YOU GO. WITH TWO FRIES, THAT'LL BE 16 EURO!

SERIOUSLY!?
A BIT MUCH, RAISING PRICES EVERY QUARTER!

IF YOU WANT THEM FOR FREE, YOU'LL HAVE TO *MARRY* ME.
HAHA, NOT IN YOUR DREAMS, JERK!

YOU'RE DISSUADING ME FROM MARRIED LIFE!
BYE! GIVE MY REGARDS TO YOUR *WIFE*!
CIAO, BELLA!

MMMM

HEY!

OUCH! CRAP!

WOW. SO "SORRY'S" ARE JUST FOR *MORONS*, HUH?

DID YOU JUST SEE THAT, LUISA?

THE NEIGHBOR'S *FRIEND WITH BENEFITS* JUST DISLOCATED MY SHOULDER!
SERIOUSLY!

ARE YOU LISTENING? WHAT'RE YOU DOING?
AREN'T YOU SICK OF PLANTING YOURSELF THERE YET? NOTHING'S GONNA HAPPEN.

GAH! I CAN'T SEE ANYTHING. I'M GETTING NEARSIGHTED.

WAIT...

PUT THESE ON...

SO? DO YOU SEE A *CLEARER* FUTURE?
HA HA. VERY FUNNY.

CAN I KEEP THEM FOR READING IF YOU DON'T NEED THEM ANYMORE?
ACTUALLY... YEAH. I GUESS I SEE WELL ENOUGH WITHOUT...

YOU'RE OUT OF LUCK IF WE CONTINUE TO SWAP PHYSICAL FEATURES LIKE THIS.

IT'S NOT GOING TO BE FUN!
IT'S FINE. IT'S NOT LIKE YOU'RE AN *OLD BIDDY!*

HONEY, AFTER YOU'RE 30, YOUR CELLS DON'T REPRODUCE AS QUICKLY...
...
EVERYTHING BREAKS DOWN. EVERYWHERE! I CAN'T WAIT TO REDISCOVER *YOUR* ABS AND GLUTES!

OKAY, GRAB YOUR FOOD. I'LL LEND YOU THE KEY, AND YOU CAN GO BACK HOME.
WE'LL MEET UP TONIGHT.

I HAVE TO GO WORK. FARID WILL KILL ME.

NO WAY! I'M COMING WITH YOU!

NO, IT'S DANGEROUS!
I DON'T THINK WE SHOULD STICK TOO CLOSELY TO EACH OTHER.

THE SENSIBLE THING TO DO IS FOR YOU TO GO HOME AND WAIT FOR ME...
YOU'RE WRONG! THIS IS AN EMERGENCY!

I DON'T WANT TO STAY HERE!

IT FEELS LIKE YOU DON'T CARE ABOUT WHAT'S GOING ON!
WHAT'LL IT CHANGE IF YOU COME WITH ME? WE HAVE NO IDEA HOW TO GET YOU BACK TO YOUR TIME AND I HAVE WORK TO DO!

WE'LL TALK ABOUT IT LATER!
I'LL BE BACK AROUND 4:00. IT WON'T BE TOO LONG.

DAMN IT!

HEY, YOU'RE ALL ALONE?
?

YOU'VE BEEN ABANDONED?

YEAH, UH... SORRY, BUT I HAVE TO GO...

IF YOU'RE LOOKING FOR YOUR UM... YOUR GIRLFRIEND, I SAW HER GO THAT WAY...
THE REDHEAD FROM LAST NIGHT...

I KNOW, BUT I WAS ACTUALLY COMING TO SEE HOW *YOU'RE*...

...DOING.

23

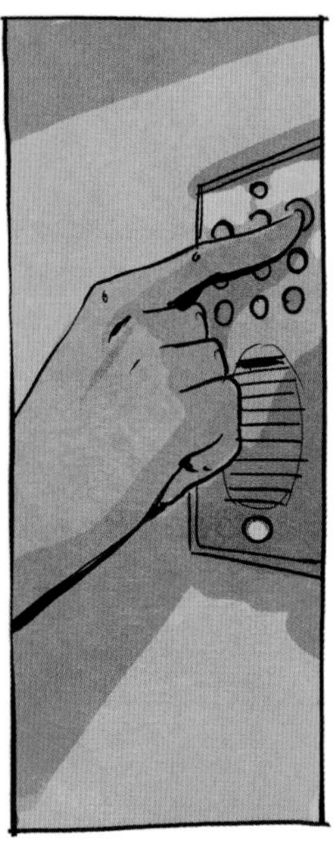

HEY...
ARE YOU
HIDING?

PRETEND I'M NOT HERE. MY COUSIN'S GOING TO *KILL* ME IF SHE KNOWS...
NONSENSE! WHAT DO YOU THINK SHE'S GOING TO SAY?

WAIT HERE. I JUST NEED TO CHECK ON SOMETHING...

HOW FAR HAVE YOU GOTTEN?
I'VE MOVED THE SPOTLIGHT A HAIR. THE LIGHT'S NOT GREAT...

WE'VE GOT ALL THE PROPS?
YEAH, JOHN WANTS THE BOTTLE MOVED CLOSER TOO.

I'M GONNA PUT A LITTLE OIL ON TOP. IT LOOKS DRAB...

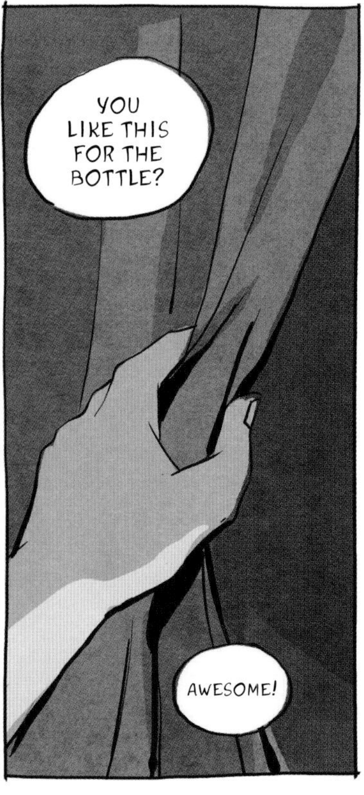
YOU LIKE THIS FOR THE BOTTLE?
AWESOME!

OKAY... THAT'S GOOD, I THINK. LET'S SHOOT!

CRAP! MY DEPTH OF FIELD IS OFF NOW...
GAH!

I'M GETTING THE 85 MM. DON'T TOUCH ANYTHING!
WE'RE *WASTING* TIME, LUISA!

FINE, FINE!

CupCake

HEY, WHAT THE HELL'S *SHE* DOING HERE?

DON'T YELL AT HER. I TOLD HER SHE COULD COME IF SHE WANTED...
SHE WANTS TO BE A PHOTOGRAPHER WHEN SHE'S OLDER, AFTER ALL!

DAMN IT! I TOLD YOU TO WAIT FOR ME AT HOME!

SO IT'S TRUE...
...YOU TAKE PICTURES OF STEAKS AND PIZZAS!

WE DO BOTTLES OF WINE, CUPCAKES, AND GOURMET FOOD, TOO.

ROVALDI
WE DO NOT DISCRIMINATE!

UM...FARID, WILL YOU LET ME SORT THIS OUT WITH MY COUSIN, PLEASE?

OKAY, OKAY, FINE...
TSSSK... I GUESS YOURS TRULY WILL TAKE CARE OF BUSINESS DURING THE DIPLOMATIC CRISIS, *AGAIN*...

WHAT DO YOU WANT...? YOU'RE DISAPPOINTED. IS THAT IT?
OKAY, YES, I AM A PROFESSIONAL. THIS IS WHAT I *DO*!

MY JOB IS TO ENHANCE WHAT I SHOOT, EVEN IF IT'S A *QUICHE*!
AND SOMETHING ELSE NOT INSIGNIFICANT, THIS WORK *PAYS MY BILLS*!

PFFF, A *FOOD* PHOTOGRAPHER... I CAN'T BELIEVE IT!

SHIT, LUISA. YOU CAN'T ALWAYS JUST DO WHATEVER YOU WANT!

LIFE IS FULL OF COMPROMISES!!

MY JOB TODAY ISN'T ONE OF THEM! I LIKE WHAT I DO NOW!
SURE! YOU DO, MAYBE!

BUT I CAN DO BETTER!
GROW UP! GET THROUGH A FEW ROUGH YEARS. THEN WE'LL TALK!

ARRGH... WHY ARE WE SO DIFFERENT, YOU AND ME?

YOU'RE RIGHT. WE ARE. AND I'M GOING BACK TO MY OWN TIME TO MAKE SURE NOT TO BECOME LIKE YOU!
THAT'S RIGHT! GO HOME! CRY TO MOM!

FUCKING KID, LEAVE!

BLÄMM

TEENAGERS ARE VERY COMPLICATED...
SO. BACK TO WORK, LUISA?

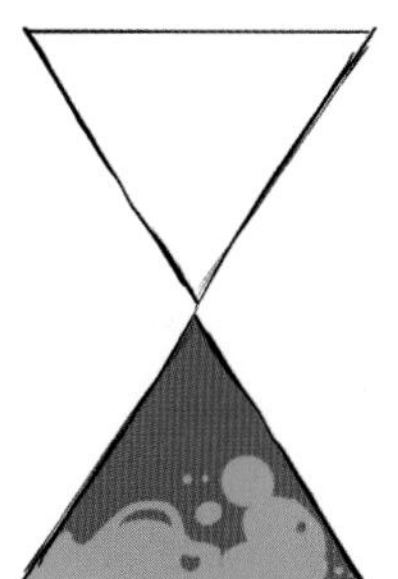

BOUCHERIE

S. BERAULT

Photos
1984 – 1998

ACADEMIE D'ORLEANS-TOUR
HIGH SCHOOL
DIPLOMA
Serie LITTERAIRE
MADEMOISELLE ARAMBOL LUISA
CHARTRES (028)
24 Avril 1980
CHARTRES

SO, LUCY BARANOV...

WHERE ARE YOU NOW...?

BASSARD : 06 40
Boris M : 01 33 48 22 13
Bolivet famille : 02 13 23
5630
Bertrand : 01 50 84 20 12
Beloto : 01 13 42 23 19
Bortolo : 06 45 15 24
BKS : 01 26-12-24 47
Benkhaoden : 02 44
Belkowen : 01 44
Bonelli D : 01 15

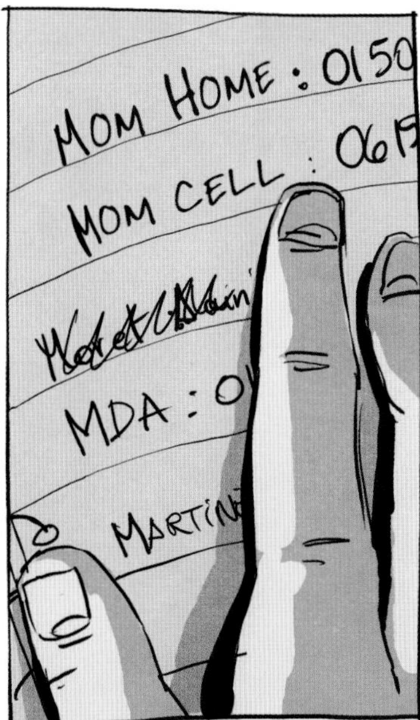
MOM HOME : 0150
MOM CELL : 06
MDA : 0
MARTIN

CRAP... NO TRACE OF HER...
BUT I HAVE MOM'S NUMBER...

YOU STILL SULKING?

YOU DO REALIZE WE ALMOST LOST A CLIENT TODAY BECAUSE OF YOUR CRAP?
PFFF, FAT CHANCE...

HEY... HAVE ANY WEED LEFT?
SERIOUSLY? ALSO IF WE SMOKE UP I'LL GET CHEWED OUT BECAUSE IT STINKS UP THE YARD. SUPPOSEDLY...

COME ON, FUCK. I NEED TO UNWIND!
OKAY, OKAY...

...

I WANT TO GET WASTED.
EXCUSE ME?
WE'RE GOING OUT TONIGHT.

NO, WAY. I'VE HAD IT! I ALREADY GOT HOME LATE LAST NIGHT FROM YOUR PLACE. I'M NOT 20 ANYMORE!
GRANDPA FARID!
AARGH!

MAN, YOU'RE IN A MOOD!
OKAY. WHERE SHOULD WE GO?

DOESN'T MATTER. I NEED TO CLEAR MY MIND AND THE FEW NEURONS I HAVE LEFT...

I'LL GO BACK TO MY PLACE, CHANGE, PICK UP THE KID AND WE'LL GO.

CRAP! WHAT'S HER PASSWORD?

TAP
TAP
TAP

INCORRECT PASSWORD
DING!

ARRRRRGH!

HEY THERE, IT'S UUUSSS!
...

TRYIN' TO SURF THE WEB?
LEAVE THE COMPUTER ALONE, HONEY. YOU'LL HAVE AMPLE TIME TO WASTE TIME ON THE INTERNET.

GET READY, WE'RE GOING OUT!
WHAT?

LOOK, I BROUGHT YOU SOME THINGS TO MAKE YOU SMILE AGAIN!

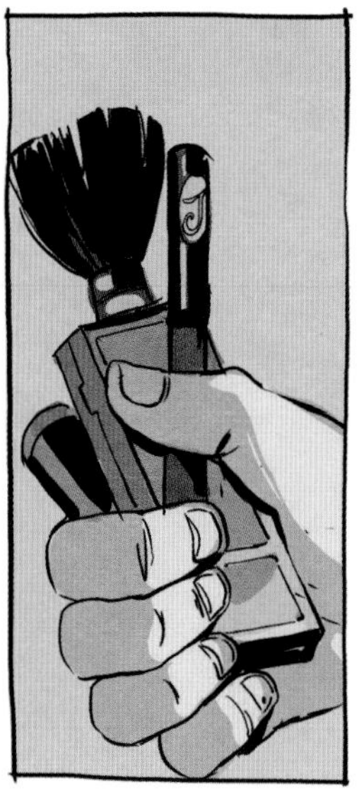

SHE SHOPLIFTED THEM...

I TRIED TO STOP HER...
I DON'T KNOW WHAT CAME OVER HER...

I'M THINKING THIS IS THE RESULT OF STRESS. OR FATIGUE.
FARID HAS DECIDED IT'S HIS JOB TO BE MY MOTHER AND LECTURE ME.

I DON'T WANT TO GO...
WHAT?
I DON'T FEEL LIKE IT...

GAH, DAMN IT! SO WHAT'S THE BIG DEAL? YOU GUYS ARE A REAL PAIN!

YOU GO MAKE YOURSELF PRETTY, GRANNY! WE'RE GOING TO FLIRT TONIGHT!
HEY!

YOU'VE GOT TWO MINUTES TO GET READY!

I'LL BE BACK!

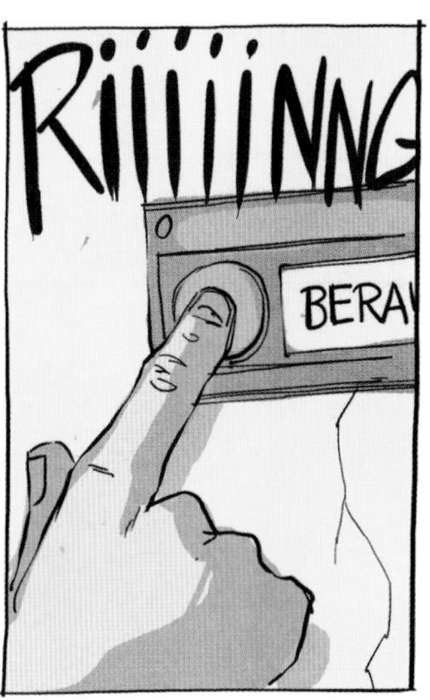
RIIIIINNG
BERA

YES?
NOPE! IT'S NOT THE DELIVERY GUY!

...?
UH... SORRY...

ACTUALLY... I WANTED TO KNOW IF...UHM... YOU WANTED TO COME WITH US AND...
WHAT?
WE'RE GOING OUT FOR A DRINK...

COME ON! PLEEEAASE!
NOW? I...

I'M *READY*...

AAAAH!
YOUR HAIR LOOKS GOOD DOWN. SEE WHAT YOU CAN DO WHEN YOU PUT YOUR MIND TO IT!

AND! SASHA'S COMING WITH US!

WHOOOO! IT'LL BE KILLLLLLER!
LET'S DANCE!
PUT ON YOUR RED SHOES AND DANCE THE BLUES

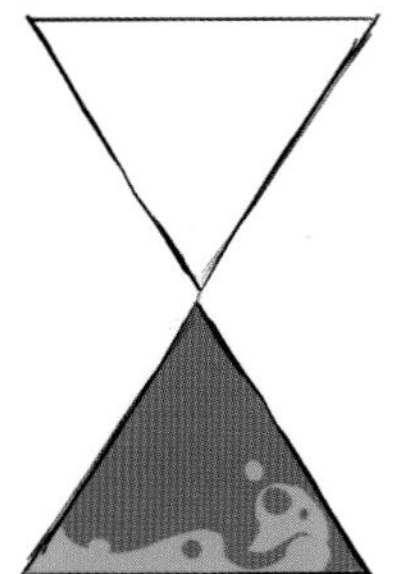

CHEZ JEANNET

SO. YOUR COUSIN'S GOING THROUGH A *ROUGH PATCH*?

DON'T KNOW. DON'T CARE.
WOW... THAT'S A MOOD. YOU'RE AS BAD AS SHE IS.

I'M DONE. TOMORROW, I'M GETTING *OUTTA* HERE. I'M GOING BACK TO MY MOTHER'S...
OH, GREAT! YOU MANAGED TO REACH HER?

NO, BUT I...
GIRLS! I'VE HAD IT!

SHE'S WIPED ME OUT! I'M TOO OLD FOR THIS, I CAN'T KEEP UP.
WHAT HAS GOTTEN INTO LUISA!?

FARIIIID! COME BACK!

COME OOOON!
SERIOUSLY...
WHAT IS SHE *ON*?

HEY! SASHA!

YOU KNOW WHAT?

NEVER MIND!

CUT IT OUT! YOU'RE EMBARRASSING US NOW!
HAHAHA! EMBARRASSED BY WHAT, EXACTLY?

EMBARRASSED BY MY HAVING SOME *FUN* FOR A CHANGE?
EMBARRASSED BY MY BEING *MYSELF*?

I'M NOT EMBARRASSED BY ANYTHING!

AND YOU SHOULDN'T BE *EITHER!*
DON'T TOUCH ME!

WE'RE GOING HOME. WE'RE DONE, LUISA. YOU'RE *DRUNK!*

GET OFF ME NOWWWW! BUNCH OF SCRUBS!
YOU'RE GOING HOME? WELL, I'M STAYING HERE!
SCRUB? HAVEN'T HEARD THAT ONE SINCE 1995.

WOOO, DAMN!

YOU CAN'T EVEN STAND UP STRAIGHT!
HOW MUCH DID YOU DRINK?
MIND YOUR OWN BEESWAX!

WHY NOT OFFER ME A CUP-O-TEA WHILE YOU'RE AT IT!

I'LL LET YOU STEW IN YOUR BAD MOOD *TOGETHER!*

SERIOUSLY... I WANT TO GO HOME!

DON'T WORRY. I GIVE HER TEN MINUTES MAX BEFORE SHE COLLAPSES AND GETS HER ASS HOME IN A TAXI.
A TAXI OR AN *AMBULANCE?*

YOU LEAVING WITH US, SASHA?

...

ASSHOLE!
SINCE WHEN D'YOU THINK YA CAN TOSS ME OUT LIKE A PIECE OF SHIT?

GO HOME!
AH, CAREFUL THERE!

DON'T TOUCH ME YOU BIG BASTARD.

THAT'S ENOUGH! YOU WANT HIM TO CALL THE COPS?
HEY, YEAHHH! I *LOVE* UNIFORMS!

LET'S SPLIT. I'M CALLING A TAXI.
I'VE SEEN ENOUGH!

HEY SASHA! YOU MAD BECAUSE YOU'RE GOING BACK EMPTY HANDED?
TSSSK, PARTY POOPER!

I...DAMN...

GOD! ARE YOU STUPID OR WHAT?! YOU JUST COOKED YOUR GOOSE WITH SASHA! YOU'RE LOSING IT.
NAAAAH....

BWAHHHHHH...

SHIT! I DON'T FEEL SO GOOD...

DON'T TOUCH ME!
OR YOU'LL *VANISH* AGAIN!

POOF! LIKE THE OTHER EVENING!
SHHHH!

OKAY, I'M ENTRUSTING THEM TO YOU. CALL ME IF YOU NEED ME!
I'M CATCHING THE LAST TRAIN.
UH... OKAY...
TAXI PARISIEN

WE NEED TO GO. SASHA'S WAITING FOR US!

I'M... I'M SORRY ABOUT THIS EVENING, LADIES....

WITH
US? OR WITH
YOURSELF?

WITH...

...WITH
MYSELF.

...

SASHA?

WE SHOULD MEET UP AGAIN, WHEN THINGS ARE...BETTER...
SURE. WHEN YOU'VE SORTED YOURSELF OUT, COME SEE ME.

AS FOR YOU...

TAKE CARE OF HER...
OKAY...

GOOD NIGHT.

OH, NO...

I'M STILL...

...CHANGING...

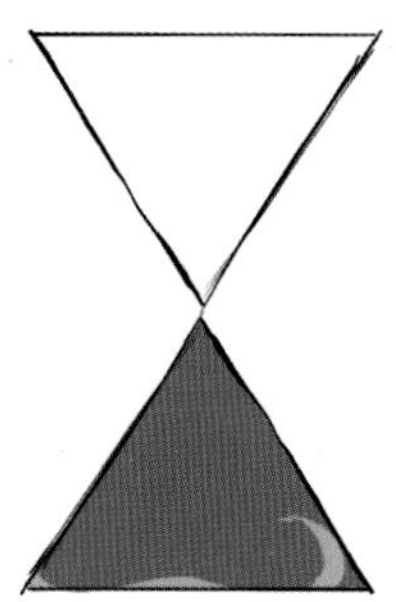

BZZZZT
BZZZZT

BZZZZT
BZZZZT
BZZZZT
MMMPH...

BZZZZT

AAAAAARGHHH!

BZZZZZT

1 NEW MESSAGE.
3 MISSED CALLS

Farid:
YOU'RE GOING TO BE LATE. IT'S 9:30! SIGNED: THE SCRUB.

CRAP!

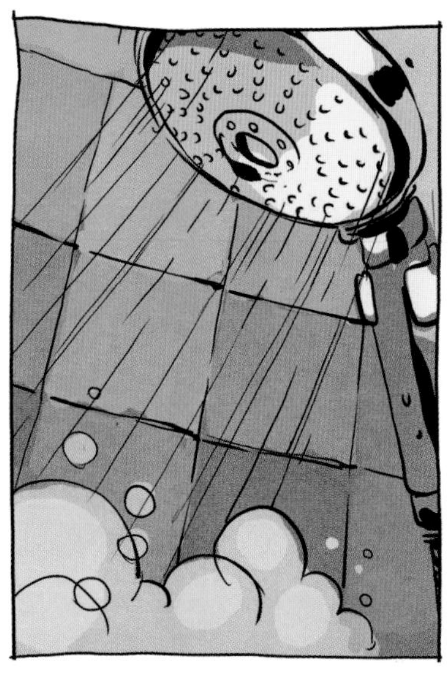

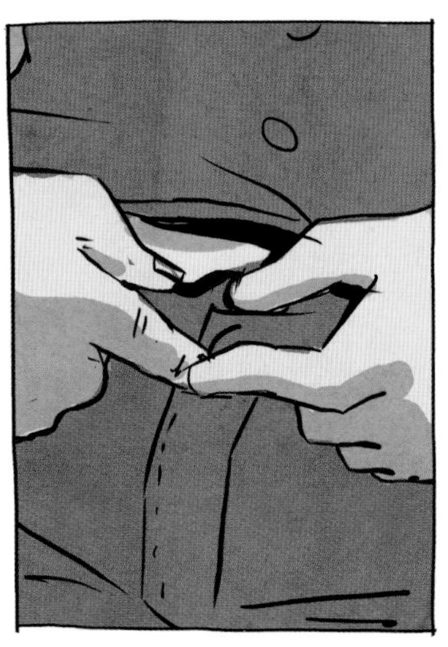

SLAM
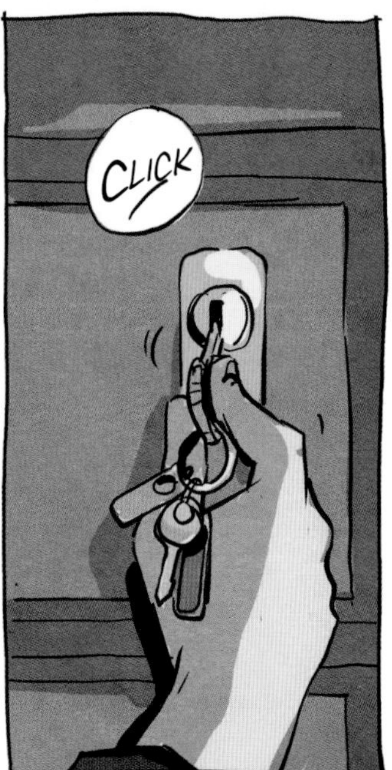
CLICK

MY HEAD...

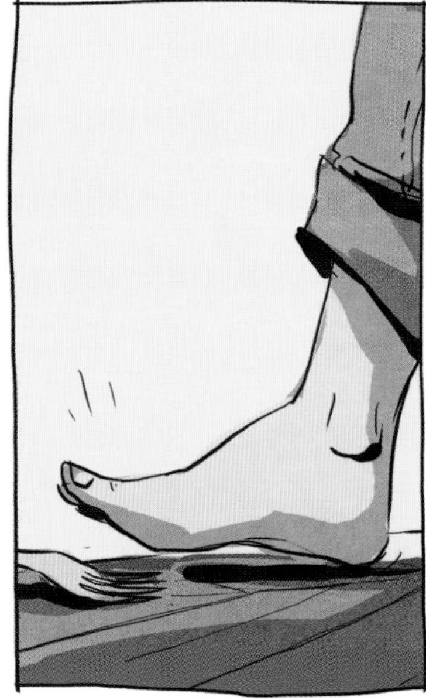

GAH!
THIS PLACE
IS A MESS!

HOLY COW!

I'M WRECKED...

...BUT I DIDN'T DRINK ANYTHING LAST NIGHT...

CRAP!

THAT IDIOT!
SHE LOCKED ME IN!

MOM:
0150125524

SASHA!

?
SASHA!

LUISA?
YES!
WEREN'T YOU SUPPOSED TO GO HOME TODAY?

YES! BUT I'M TRAPPED!

HANG ON, I'M COMING!

LUISA. I'M HERE. WHAT HAPPENED?

IT'S MY COUSIN...
SHE RACED OFF TO WORK AND *LOCKED* ME IN!

YOU SHOULD'VE SLEPT AT MY PLACE YESTERDAY...
NO... NEVER MIND...

IT'LL BE OKAY...
SHE WON'T BE LONG.

HONESTLY...
I DON'T KNOW WHICH OF YOU TWO IS THE TEENAGER IN ALL THIS...

WHAT YOU WERE PLAYING WAS PRETTY.
THANKS.

WHEN I HAVE TIME BETWEEN SESSIONS, I LIKE TO MESS AROUND ON MY LITTLE KEYBOARD...

IT MUST BE LIKE TAKING PRETTY PICTURES WHEN YOU SPEND YOUR TIME TAKING PUBLICITY PHOTOS...

KIND OF LIKE A BREATH OF FRESH AIR.

YOU AND I NEED TO TALK ABOUT SOMETHING.
YE... YES?

WHAT'S THAT PHOTO I FOUND IN MY MAILBOX?

...

I KNOW YOU PUT IT THERE.
IT'S A BIT OF A CRAZY MOVE FOR YOUR COUSIN.

BUT, SHE'S THE ONE WHO HAD THE CRAZY IDEA TO TAKE THE PICTURE... I THOUGHT IT WAS BEAUTIFUL...

I THOUGHT *YOU* WERE BEAUTIFUL...

SORRY... THAT'S STUPID, RIGHT?

NO.. IT'S...
...TOUCHING.

YOU KNOW... IF YOU WEREN'T SO YOUNG...

IT'S FUNNY YOU'RE REALLY MATURE FOR YOUR AGE, AND AT THE SAME TIME, YOU HAVE THAT ASSERTIVENESS, THAT ANGER...

...THAT *AUDACITY* THAT TEENAGERS HAVE...

IT'S SEDUCTIVE.

I DON'T KNOW...
I DON'T KNOW WHAT I AM ANYMORE.

OR WHAT YOU MIGHT BECOME...

HEY, SASHA...
YES?

I THINK I'M LIKE YOU.
IN WHAT WAY?

WELL... *GIRLS*, YOU KNOW...

OH, THAT!? HAHAHA!

WELL, YOU'RE STILL A LITTLE YOUNG TO BE SURE, BUT IT'S GOOD NOT TO EXCLUDE THE POSSIBILITY...

MANY PEOPLE WHO SUPPRESS WHO THEY ARE AT YOUR AGE...
THE EXPERIENCES YOU HAVE LATER ON WILL HELP YOU SEE THINGS MORE CLEARLY...

I-I KISSED A FRIEND LAST WEEK...

OK. AND... HOW DID IT MAKE YOU FEEL?

IT WAS AN ACCIDENT, BUT I THINK IT WAS WHAT I WANTED DEEP DOWN .
I THINK I LOVE HER.

WHAT'S WORRYING YOU THEN?
IT'S HARD. IT'S AS IF, BACK THERE, EVERYONE'S AGAINST "THAT." NO ONE LIKES LUCY.
MOM DOESN'T WANT ME TO SEE HER...IF SHE KNEW, SHE'D BE FURIOUS...

IS THAT WHY YOU RAN AWAY?

...

IT'S A CLASSIC STORY, HONEY...

I'LL TELL YOU A SLIGHTLY DIFFERENT ONE IF YOU'D LIKE...

WHEN I WAS YOUR AGE, A FRIEND OF MINE WAS CRAZY ABOUT ONE OF HER TEACHERS...

AT THE TIME, SHE DIDN'T UNDERSTAND WHAT WAS HAPPENING TO HER. IT SEEMED HUGE NEXT TO HER FRIENDS' TRIVIAL BOYFRIENDS.

IT WAS SO MUCH STRONGER THAN THEIR MECHANICAL MAKE OUT SESSIONS...

SHE FELT A SURGE OF DESIRE AT EVERY LESSON. IT WENT FAR BEYOND MERE ADMIRATION.

I THINK IT WAS A KIND OF *REVELATION* TO HER.
WHEN YOU BECOME AWARE OF THIS KIND OF THING...

...WHEN YOU BEGIN TO ACCEPT THAT IT CAN HAPPEN TO YOU...
IT'S AS IF YOU'RE DOING YOUR OWN COMING-OUT TO YOURSELF.

THE FIRST ONE, WHICH WILL LEAD TO OTHERS MUCH LATER...
...AND THE *HARDEST* ONE...

WHAT HAPPENED BETWEEN THE TEACHER AND YOUR FRIEND?
ABSOLUTELY NOTHING!

I WAS SATISFIED WITH DREAMING LIKE A *FOOL*...

SHE WAS OLDER THAN ME. I WAS ONLY 14...

LUISA, IF YOU GIVE YOURSELF PERMISSION TO LOVE AND DESIRE IN THAT WAY, IT'S ALREADY A VICTORY FOR YOU. YOU'LL BE HAPPY...
WE DON'T *CHOOSE* THE PEOPLE WE FALL FOR, BUT WE *DO* CHOOSE WHETHER TO ACCEPT THESE FEELINGS OR NOT.

BY TELLING ME YOUR STORY, IT'S LIKE YOU'VE ALREADY MADE THE CHOICE TO ACCEPT THEM.

!
WHEN YOU GO BACK HOME, YOU NEED TO TALK TO YOUR MOTHER SO YOU CAN WORK THINGS OUT.

AND IF...THEY DON'T?
GIVE HER TIME...

SHE JUST WANTS TO PROTECT YOU FROM SOMETHING SHE DOESN'T UNDERSTAND, OR UNDERSTANDS POORLY. BUT NO MATTER WHAT, DON'T SUPPRESS YOUR FEELINGS...
...AND DON'T LET HER HOLD YOU BACK, OKAY?

YOU KNOW THAT IF YOU WEREN'T SO OLD...

HEEEEEY! YOU'RE A LITTLE DEVIL!

TILILILILILILI
TILILILILILI
SORRY, THE PHONE'S RINGING. MAYBE IT'S MY COUSIN. I'LL BE RIGHT BACK.

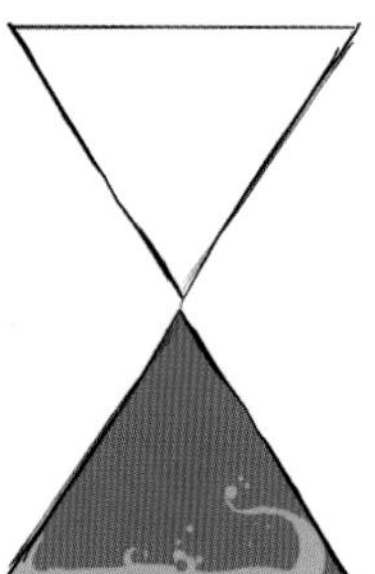

TILILILILILIIIIIIT

BEEEP
LUISA? IT'S MOM.

IT'S BEEN SO LONG SINCE WE'VE SEEN EACH OTHER. THERE'S AN EXHIBIT AT THE GRAND PALAIS... I'M GOING THERE IN A BIT...MAYBE YOU'D LIKE TO MEET ME THERE?

ANYWAY, IT'S UP TO YOU, OKAY? LOVE.
BEEEP

MOM!

HELLO, MISS SASHA! HOW ARE YOU?
GOOD... I WAS JUST GOING BACK IN...
YOU'RE BACK TO BEING FORMAL?

YOU WERE MORE... INTIMATE, YESTERDAY...
YES... WELL, I'VE HAD A ROUGH DAY.

YEAH, I WAS JUST TALKING TO YOUR COUSIN. SHE'S HAVING A HARD DAY TOO.

YOU LEFT HER LOCKED UP. AND ALONE.

BLOODY HELL, WHAT EXACTLY ARE YOU DOING?

I WANTED TO CALL MOM!
WHAT?! HOW?
SHE LEFT A MESSAGE. SHE'S GOING TO A MUSEUM. I WANT TO *TALK* TO HER. I'M GOING TO MEET HER.

STOP IT! DROP THAT!

HEEY!

SHIT!
THINGS ARE NOT OKAY!

YOU HAVE TO GET OUT OF HERE NOW!
LOOK, WE'RE EXCHANGING. THIS ISN'T NORMAL. IT'S DANGEROUS!

I'M LEAVING!
AND I'M LOOKING FORWARD TO IT!

YOU'RE AN IDIOT. I DON'T DESERVE YOUR LIFE.

I DON'T LIKE YOUR WORK!
YOU'RE ALONE. YOU'RE ASHAMED OF YOUR FEELINGS!

YOU DON'T TALK TO MOM ANYMORE AND YOU HAVEN'T EVEN KEPT IN TOUCH WITH MY FRIENDS!
WHAT ARE YOU TALKING ABOUT?

I SEE, AGNES!
I'M TALKING ABOUT *LUCY!*
WHY ISN'T SHE YOUR FRIEND ANYMORE?

PEOPLE GROW UP. THINGS CHANGE. YOU LOSE TOUCH. IT HAPPENS...YOU FIND OTHER FRIENDS...

YEAH WELL SHE, SHE WAS *IMPORTANT* TO ME!
SUUURE, SHE WAS SO IMPORTANT THAT YOU WERE A COWARD WITH HER.

I DON'T KNOW WHAT BECAME OF HER AFTER FANNY'S COUSINS INSULTED HER, RIGHT IN FRONT OF ME.
SHE WENT HOME AND I NEVER DARED TO SPEAK TO HER AGAIN. I WAS SO ASHAMED THAT I'D DONE NOTHING.

A FEW WEEKS LATER, SHE AND HER PARENTS MOVED AWAY. I ALWAYS FELT A LITTLE RESPONSIBLE FOR THEIR LEAVING.

SHE MUST HAVE *HATED* ME. I THOUGHT I'D HURT HER ENOUGH AS IT WAS...
I STILL FEEL BAD ABOUT IT.

SHE LEFT BECAUSE OF *ME?*
IT'S ALWAYS BUGGED ME. IT'S LIKE SHE'S ON MY CONSCIENCE.

I SHOULD'VE LISTENED TO MOM AND LEFT LUCY *ALONE* INSTEAD OF GOING OVER TO BUG HER, INSTEAD OF...

I'M GOING TO GO AND TALK TO MOM. YOU AREN'T TELLING ME EVERYTHING...

NO!

I'M GOING TO MEET MOM. YOU'RE STAYING HERE!
HEY!

SBAMM

HOLY SHIT!

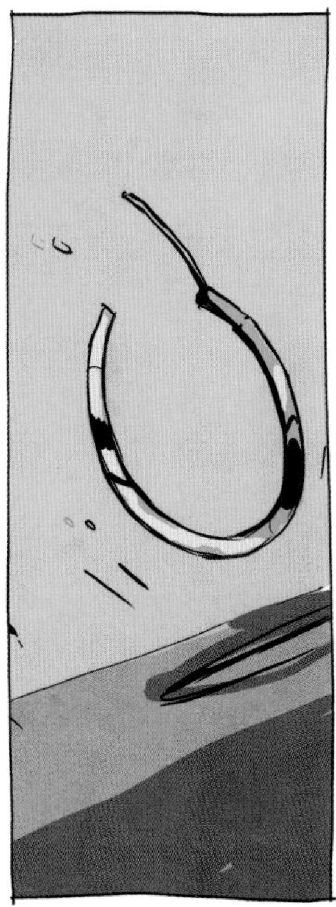

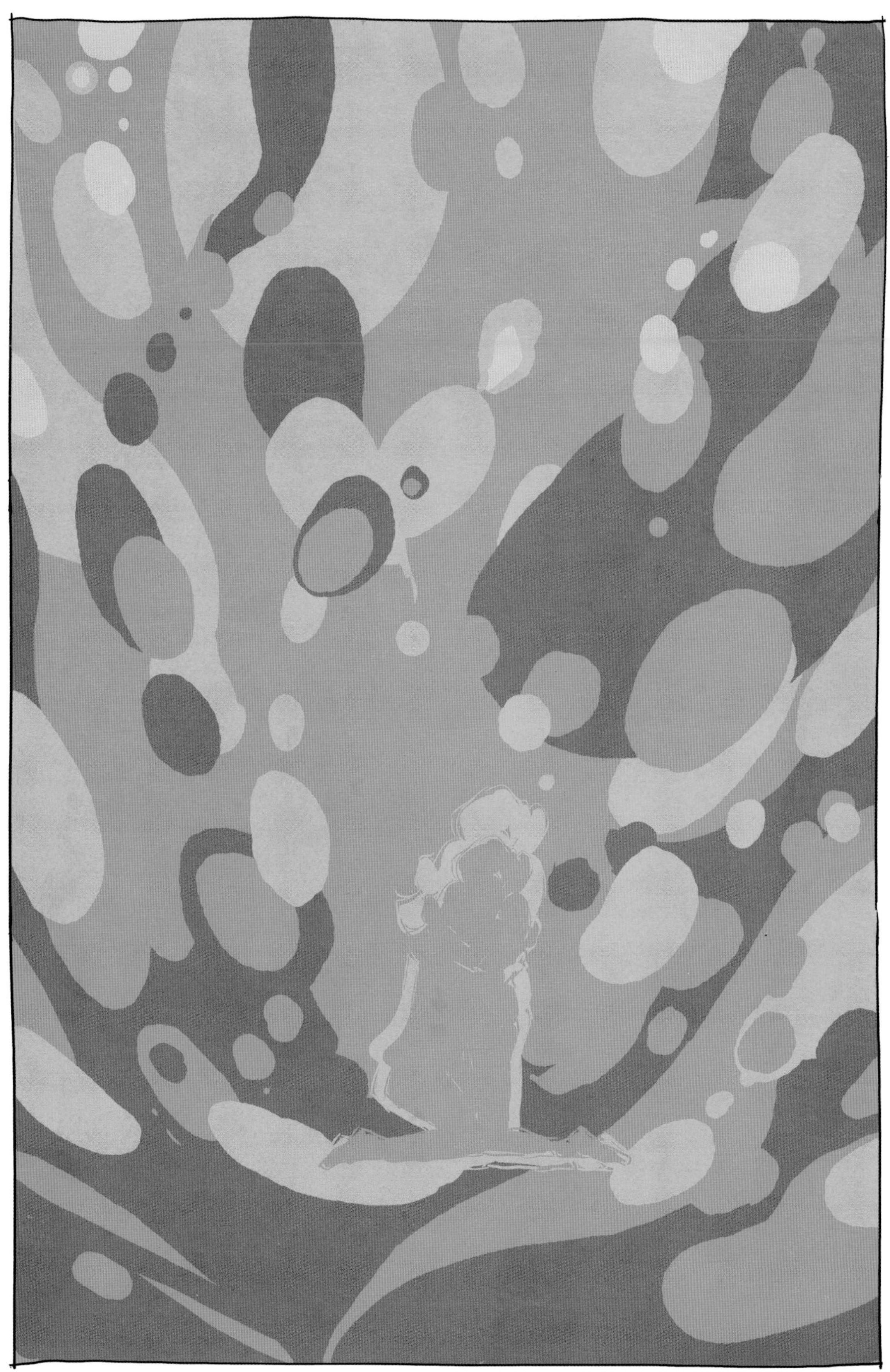

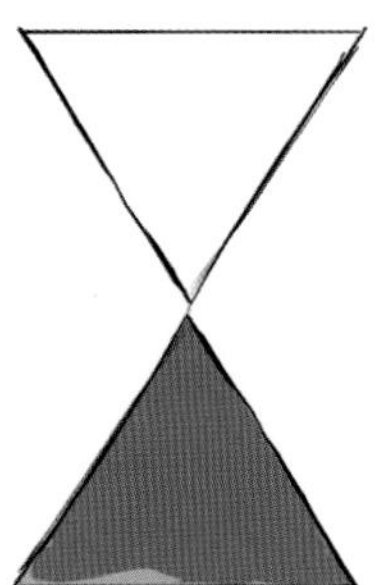

SHE'S GONE?

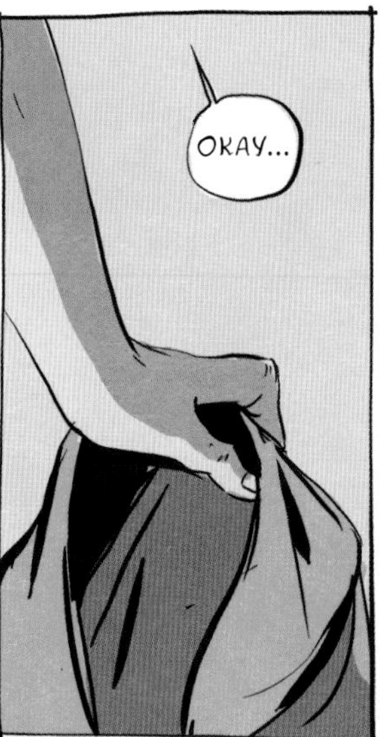
OKAY...

I'M GETTING OUT OF HERE...

HEY! LUISA! IS EVERYTHING OKAY?
DON'T WORRY... EVERYTHING'S BACK TO NORMAL.

I HAVE TO GO.
WAIT A SEC...WHAT ABOUT YOUR COUSIN?

SHE'LL CALL YOU!
AND I WILL TOO, I PROMISE!

SEE YOU SOON, SASHA!

TAXI
PARISIEN

TO THE GRAND PALAIS, PLEASE!
YES, MA'AM!

MA'AM?
MISS, IF YOU PREFER...

...

YOU WANT TO GET DROPPED OFF HERE?
YES, PLEASE.

THAT'LL BE 17 EURO.

HERE YOU GO!

HEY!

AAAARGH!

WHAT... IS THIS EXHIBIT?

MOM?

YOU'RE LATE...

I KNOW... I DIDN'T KNOW WHERE YOU WERE.
AS ABSENTMINDED AS A TEENAGER, MY DAUGHTER...

I WON'T HOLD IT AGAINST YOU. FOR ONCE YOU'RE HERE...

I THOUGHT YOU WERE SCREENING MY CALLS AND THAT YOU WOULDN'T COME, AS USUAL...
...

...I DON'T WANT TO GET UPSET. I JUST WANT THE TWO OF US TO TALK...
MMOKAY...

SO YOU WANT ME TO GET ALL WORKED UP...

WHAT ARE YOU ANNOUNCING, THEN?

YOU'VE FINALLY MET A MAN?
SOMEONE YOU WON'T BREAK UP WITH AFTER TWO WEEKS?

WOW. YOU'RE *OBSESSED!*
ALWAYS FLITTING AROUND! HOW DO YOU EXPECT TO BE TAKEN SERIOUSLY?

WHAT IS IT YOU WANT TO TALK ABOUT?

...

DO YOU REMEMBER THAT GIRL?
...LUCY BARONOV?

THE GIRL YOU OFTEN WENT TO SEE WHEN YOU WERE A TEENAGER?

YES, OF COURSE, I REMEMBER HER... A TROUBLED GIRL.
DID SHE REALLY MOVE AWAY?

YES...I THINK HER FATHER GOT A JOB ELSEWHERE...
THE POOR PARENTS...SOMEHOW... I FELT SORRY FOR THEM...

DIRTY DYKE
WHORE!
THEY WERE NEVER LEFT ALONE... AND THERE WAS A LOT OF GOSSIP IN THE NEIGHBORHOOD ABOUT THEIR DAUGHTER...
"WHO" NEVER LEFT THEM ALONE?

PEOPLE.
PEOPLE, IN GENERAL.

THEIR DAUGHTER CAUSED THEM SO MANY PROBLEMS, ALWAYS GETTING HERSELF NOTICED, PROVOKING.
DYKE
I WAS RIGHT TO WARN YOU AGAINST HER AT THE TIME...

SHE DIDN'T DO ANYTHING WRONG.
SHE WAS A *BAD INFLUENCE* ON YOU, THAT'S ALL.

I DIDN'T WANT YOU TO END UP LIKE YOUR POOR AUNT AURELIA...
WHAT ARE YOU TALKING ABOUT? WHAT'S THE DEAL WITH AURELIA?

SINCE THIS IS A DAY FOR SECRETS...

YOUR AUNT CAUSED A LOT OF TALK ABOUT HERSELF IN THE FAMILY...
...BEFORE THE SCANDAL.

AT THE END OF
THE 70S, SHE MET
A YOUNG WOMAN...
SHE INTRODUCED HER
TO US AS A FRIEND...BUT
SHE HAD FALLEN DEEPLY
IN LOVE WITH HER.

YOU
CAN IMAGINE
THE FAMILY'S
REACTION.

LATER, AURELIA'S
LOVER SUCCUMBED TO HER
FAMILY'S PRESSURE AND
MARRIED A MAN.

AS FOR AURELIA,
SHE DECIDED TO ACCEPT
HER HOMOSEXUALITY.

AND SHE HAD A
FALLING OUT WITH
YOUR FATHER'S FAMILY,
INCLUDING ME...

SHE HAD NO ONE ELSE AFTER HER BREAK-UP.

YEARS PASSED. I *NEVER* FORGAVE HER FOR NOT COMING BACK TO US.

OR AT LEAST TO ME, FOR I'D CONSIDERED HER LIKE A *SISTER*...

HER FEELINGS GOT THE BEST OF HER...

...THE WHOLE SITUATION MADE HER VERY SAD...

...IN SOME WAYS, I THINK SHE DIED FROM IT...

AND AS IF TO *TAUNT* ME, SHE DECIDED TO BEQUEATH HER APARTMENT TO YOU...
I DIDN'T WANT YOU TO FALL INTO THE SAME TRAP. I WANTED TO PROTECT YOU FROM ALL THAT.
I FELT THAT WITH THIS LUCY, THERE WAS A SIMILAR KIND OF ATTRACTION STARTING UP BETWEEN THE TWO OF YOU AND THAT WORRIED ME. I THOUGHT IT DANGEROUS.
ARAMBOL
YOUR AUNT NEVER RECOVERED. I DIDN'T WANT YOU TO LIVE THROUGH THE SAME THING, CUTTING ALL TIES WITH US, WITH YOUR FAMILY. IT'S *EASY* TO UNDERSTAND, ISN'T IT?

MOM...

YES?

WHAT KILLED AURELIA WASN'T THE FACT THAT SHE LOVED A WOMAN BUT RATHER THE FACT THAT THE PEOPLE *CLOSE* TO HER REJECTED THAT LOVE.

REJECTED BY OTHERS, BY OUR FAMILY, BY HER FRIEND'S FAMILY...
...

IT'S THE SAME REJECTION THAT MADE LUCY MOVE!

TRULY.

IF I TOLD YOU TODAY THAT I FEEL CLOSER TO MY DEAD AUNT THAN TO YOU, EVEN THOUGH I BARELY KNEW HER...

YOU'D THINK THAT WAS PARADOXICAL, WOULDN'T YOU?
YES, AND VERY UNFAIR.

I'LL TELL YOU, EVEN THOUGH I FEEL VERY CLOSE TO HER, THERE'S A DETAIL THAT MAKES A HUGE DIFFERENCE BETWEEN HER AND ME.
OF COURSE THERE IS: YOU PREFER MEN...

NO. BUT I'M LUCKIER THAN HER, IN SOME WAYS.

AND I COULDN'T CARE LESS ABOUT OTHER PEOPLE'S REJECTION...
YOU *DON'T* LIKE MEN?

GAH! I HAVEN'T GOT A CLUE!
WHAT I KNOW IS THAT I'M ABLE TO FALL IN LOVE WITH WOMEN!

I'VE DENIED WHO I WAS WITH YOUR *IDIOCY* OF WANTING TO PROTECT ME FROM MY DESIRES *AT ALL COSTS.*

YOU CAN'T IMAGINE THE EMOTIONAL STANDSTILL I'VE BEEN AT ALL THESE YEARS!

SO YES, IT'S ENTIRELY POSSIBLE THAT DESPITE THE SUFFOCATING EMOTIONAL GUARDRAIL THAT YOU SET UP, I'M ATTRACTED TO *CHICKS* AND SORRY, BUT YOU CAN'T DO MUCH ABOUT IT...

...
WHAT'RE YOU GOING TO DO? WHAT YOU DID WITH MY AUNT? REJECT THE IDEA? REJECT ME?

VERY WELL.

YOU'VE CHOSEN TO BE LIKE THAT. BUT I DIDN'T *CHOOSE* ANYTHING. YOU CAN'T IMPOSE *ANYTHING* ON ME!

I'M NOT CHOOSING. YOU ARE CHOOSING.

YOU CAN *STILL* CHOOSE TO ACCEPT *ME*...

...

OKAY...

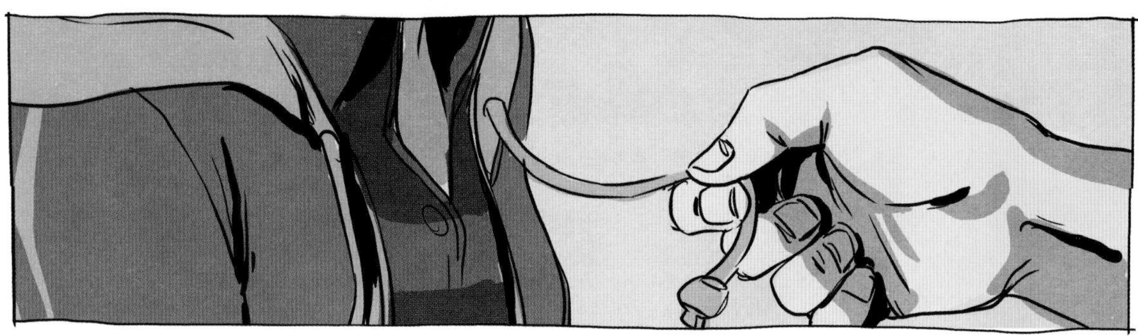

< Directory >
Sasha (Neighbor)
06 54 98 77 04

THE END

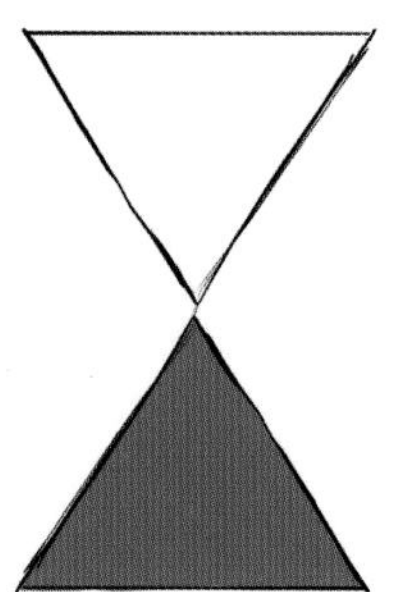

LUISA, IS THAT YOU?
YOU'RE *PUSHING* IT! I SAID 6 O'CLOCK! I'VE BEEN WORRIED SICK!

IT'S NOT MY FAULT! I DIDN'T NOTICE THE TIME!

CMAUREL
2016.